THE
EARLY
CHURCH
AND THE COMING GREAT CHURCH

THE
EARLY
CHURCH

AND THE COMING GREAT CHURCH

JOHN KNOX

ABINGDON PRESS
NEW YORK · NASHVILLE

95- B2083

G

THE WILLIAM HENRY HOOVER LECTURESHIP ON CHRISTIAN UNITY
The Disciples Divinity House of the University of Chicago

The William Henry Hoover Lectureship on Christian Unity was established by the Disciples Divinity House at the University of Chicago in 1945. Resources for the lectureship are a trust fund established in the amount of $50,000 some years prior to his death by Mr. W. H. Hoover, of North Canton, Ohio. The purpose of the fund was designated as the promotion of Christian unity, a cause for which Mr. Hoover demonstrated a lifelong interest. Originally the fund had been used for initiating publications, notably periodicals which have since become well established. With the successful launching of these enterprises it was decided that the cause of Christian unity could best be served by establishing at a major university center a lectureship on Christian unity, no such lectureship having yet come into existence. The Disciples Divinity House of the University of Chicago was asked to accept Mr. Hoover's trust for the purposes of sponsoring a lectureship on Christian unity.

The intention of those establishing the lectureship is that each lecturer shall be a distinguished Christian churchman of this or some other country, whose experience, research and knowledge eminently qualify him to discuss the problem of Christian unity and to make a positive contribution toward closer co-operation of the many Christian denominations and the ultimate unity of the church of Christ.

A series of lectures is normally to be given annually and to be published as the Hoover Lectures.

THE EARLY CHURCH AND THE COMING GREAT CHURCH

Copyright MCMLV by Pierce & Washabaugh

Library of Congress Catalog Card Number: 55-6765

Scripture quotations unless otherwise noted are from the Revised Standard Version of the Bible and are copyright 1946 and 1952 by the Division of Christian Education of the National Council of the Churches of Christ in the U.S.A.

SET UP, PRINTED, AND BOUND BY THE
PARTHENON PRESS, AT NASHVILLE,
TENNESSEE, UNITED STATES OF AMERICA

TO

CHARLES CLAYTON MORRISON

ὃς προστάτης πολλῶν ἐγενήθη

καὶ ἐμοῦ αὐτοῦ

FOREWORD

The question with which we shall be concerned in the following pages is: How normative is early Christianity? That the experience of the primitive church has a peculiar relevance—may we say authority?—for all subsequent periods and specifically for our own is readily acknowledged by us all, and we are constantly appealing to that experience both in justifying the beliefs and practices of our several denominations and in discussing the nature of the united church for which we strive and wait. But does the primitive church give infallible and adequate guidance? Are there limits to its relevance and authority? If so, how shall we define these limits? These are questions of great importance for the ecumenical enterprise, the answers to which will probably not be altogether clear until the goal of unity has been actually attained. Meantime, however, there is value in thinking about them and in trying to formulate answers as clear and definite as possible. I am as aware as any critic can be of how lacking in clarity and definiteness—not to say truth—the final conclusions of this book may be. I am hoping only to make a contribution to a discussion in which I have much more to learn than to teach.

I need to thank the following friends for their willingness to read all or portions of my manuscript: Norman Pittenger, Wilhelm Pauck, Walter Horton, and Cyril Richardson. Needless to say, none of them is to be held responsible in the least degree for the faults of this work, but their suggestions and criticisms

7

were exceedingly helpful. I am also indebted to another friend, Theodore O. Wedel, who besides giving me much through his book *The Coming Great Church,* has permitted me to use its title in naming my own.

Several notes of a lexical kind need to be included here. The term "early church" is often used to designate the church of the first four or five centuries; but I have used it, in a narrower way, as a synonym of "primitive church," the church of the New Testament period. I have not been consistent in my use of "he" or "it" in references to the Spirit; sometimes, as in the New Testament, the context seems to require the impersonal pronoun. The problem of whether the term "catholic" should be spelled with a lower-case or a capital "C" is a perennial one. Because in this book the term is never used in the broad, general sense of "universal," but always to designate a particular kind of ecclesiastical order and life, I have decided to spell it consistently with the capital. Nowhere have I used the word in the popular, but inaccurate, sense of merely or specifically Roman Catholic, although the Roman Church and its members are never left out of consideration. The coming great church must include us all. The words "Protestant" and "Catholic," while suggesting different emphases or tendencies, are not necessarily mutually exclusive terms.

Although this book has been prepared primarily for publication, several of its chapters contain lectures which I have been invited to give at the University of Chicago. I am deeply grateful to those responsible for the administering of the Hoover Lectureship for the honor of this invitation and, especially to Dr. Charles Clayton Morrison and Dean Barnett Blakemore of the Disciples Divinity House, for helpful counsel.

John Knox

CONTENTS

10

WHEN WAS
THE CHURCH UNITED?

THE CHRISTIAN CHURCH IN OUR GENERATION is struggling desperately with what is seen to be a crucial problem in its own life—the problem of disunion. The mere proliferation of denominations within Protestantism, even where there is full mutual esteem and where no denial of communion is involved, is itself a serious, and strangely obstinate, problem. But the disunion that most acutely concerns us is that deeper separation among Christians, wherever it exists and whether it is based on race, creed, or cult, which in effect makes fellowship impossible and often sets church against church. How—we find ourselves asking—can we longer suffer the pain and the shame of this terrible schism and conflict? How can the church act for the healing of the nations when it must nurse such deep wounds in its own body? How can the church, so deeply divided, make its influence felt in the mores of societies and the policies of nations? How can it bear witness to Christ? Indeed, how can it be regarded as the church at all?

These are questions of critical urgency, and I should be distressed if anything I may say should have the effect of lessening our concern about them. I know that we have reason to be, and must needs be, much more profoundly and painfully concerned about them than we are. At the same time, we should be

11

mistaken if we supposed that the disunion of Christendom were a new, or merely modern, fact. Though the solution may never before have been so earnestly sought, and so desperately needed, the problem is as old as Christianity itself. Schism did not begin with the Reformation. The medieval church was deeply divided as between East and West long before the rift became definite and fixed in the eleventh century, and there were constant or recurrent conflict, revolt, and schism within each area. The ancient church—that is, the church between the second and fifth centuries —came much nearer to being united, but no reader of Professor S. L. Greenslade's book *Schism in the Early Church*[1] will be under the illusion that unity was fully achieved. Indeed, the whole history of Christianity under one of its aspects is without any question a history of controversy, division, and often bitter conflict. Only one who begins by identifying Christianity with one particular strain or segment of the history can deny this, and even he would have to be amazingly agile and ingenious to make his case. Our common phrase "the reunion of Christendom" is, strictly speaking, erroneous. There has never been a time when the church could be truly said to be united.

But, someone says, you have forgotten about the New Testament period, the first age of the church; surely then the church was one. So we have often supposed. The early church—the church of the first and early second century—has appeared to be our norm in this respect, as in so many others. But only a very superficial study of our sources should be enough to dispel this illusion. However the goal of the ecumenical movement is to be reached, it will not be by the simple return to the primitive church. To be sure, we do not find there organized systems of churches, like the churches of the East and West in the Middle

[1] New York: Harper & Bros., 1953.

Ages, or like our modern denominations—perhaps not in communion with one another, certainly sharply separated from one another—each with its own set of traditions and usages and with its intimate mutual "intramural" loyalties. In a word, there were no "churches" in the sense of limited organized associations of congregations.[2] But on the other hand, it would not have been possible to speak of "the church" in the sense of an inclusive organization of congregations. Nor does one find simply a radical and consistent independency. The situation was in flux: congregations were related more or less closely with other congregations, sharing in varying degrees in common traditions, beliefs, and practices, acknowledging the validity of some of the same norms and the authority of some of the same persons; but there was wide diversity in both cult and faith, and signs of tension and of actual division, both within and among congregations, are not lacking.

This subject is too important for our purposes to be dealt with here. The whole of the first chapter will be devoted to demonstrating the existence of diversity and division in the early church and to showing something of their nature and extent. But if I may be permitted to anticipate this demonstration, it will perhaps be useful at this stage to raise and briefly answer two questions which logically follow from it: (1) How, in the face of many indications of division and conflict, has the picture of the early church as a model of unity and peace been able to maintain itself? (2) Why is it important for the ecumenical movement that the illusory character of this picture be recognized and acknowledged? The points I shall now make in answer to these questions will all come in for larger discussion in various connections later in this book.

[2] For an important discussion of the denomination—its essential character and its essential incompatibility with the ecumenical ideal—see the Hoover Lectures of 1951, Charles Clayton Morrison, *The Unfinished Reformation* (New York: Harper & Bros., 1953), pp. 26-73.

To the question about how the usual picture of early Christian unity has managed to survive, the first answer is undoubtedly: Because we want it to be so. A culture always tends to idealize its past and often regards its primitive epoch as its golden age. This is particularly likely to be true of religious cultures and, most likely of all perhaps, of religious cultures like Judaism and Christianity, which trace their origins to great revealing events in the past. The very fact that we now seek the visible unity of the church with such deep desire makes us seek for this same unity in the primitive church; and it is easier to overlook the evidences of its absence there than it is to overcome the obstacles to its presence here. It is also true that the task of finding a feasible and authoritative pattern of unity is greatly simplified, if not indeed already performed for us, if we can actually observe the unified church in the New Testament. The wish thus becomes father to the thought.

Another source of error is the emphasis the New Testament itself lays from time to time upon the unity of the church; for example, the affirmation of Eph. 4:4-5 that there is "one body and one Spirit, . . . one Lord, one faith, one baptism." But such affirmations are obviously to be understood as reflecting an actual situation, not of unity, but the reverse. The affirmation of unity needs to be made because the unity itself is being, in practice at least, denied. We are constantly in danger of supposing that the exalted conceptions of the great biblical teachers were not only shared by the rank and file of the community but also actually embodied in its life. A few moments of reflection, however, are enough to make us see not only that this is expecting far too much of ordinary men, but also that it was usually their very failure in insight or character which called forth the exalted utterances of the prophets.

We are also deceived perhaps by the very existence of the New

14

Testament. Here are twenty-seven books, by something like a dozen early Christian authors, embodying a considerable variety of views, reflecting a rather diversified background of community life—and yet here they are together, united in one collection, all essential parts of one book. But let us not forget that the canon was the product, not of the first and early second centuries, but of the late second and early third. The primitive church produced the several books; it did not produce the New Testament. The New Testament canon is not to be understood as a sign of the visible unity of the primitive church; rather, it was a consciously created instrument of the post-apostolic church for the achieving of a visible unity among the many groups, with their varied and often conflicting ideas and practices, which primitive Christianity had bequeathed to it.

Our second question was: Why should we emphasize this matter of the diversity and disjunctiveness of early Christianity? Granted that the picture of primitive harmony and union may be somewhat illusory, is anything gained by demonstrating this? Can this demonstration be other than discouraging and destructive so far as the ecumenical enterprise is concerned? By way of answer to such questions I would make three points.

First, our recognition of the fact that the church, which has never been fully united in a visible unity, was not thus united in the Apostolic Age, will keep us from interpreting the goal of the ecumenical movement as being simply the restoration of the forms and usages of the early church.[3] Every Christian group, almost, if not quite, without exception, has assumed that it could justify its beliefs and practices by the New Testament and that no authoritative belief could be justified in any other way. Most denominations have regarded the early church

[3] See the illuminating discussion of this danger in Morrison, *op. cit.*, pp. 130-58, 175-78.

15

as being not only the minimal norm which must not be violated but also the adequate model which needs only to be followed. We have not been content to say, "Nothing can be true or right which contravenes the faith and practice of the primitive church." We have insisted on saying, "Nothing can be true or right which did not belong to the faith and practice of the primitive church." The consequence is that we tend either to repudiate what would otherwise be acceptable and useful forms, because we cannot find them authoritatively exemplified in the early church, or to distort the sources in order to give these same forms an apparent validation. In both cases we are attributing to the actual practices of primitive Christianity an authority, as well as a consistency, they did not possess.

We are also making more difficult the achievement of church union. The coming great church cannot be a church which simply perpetuates a single strain in early Christianity or acknowledges the authority of only one segment of the apostolic church or of only one stage in its development. But it is equally true—and even more obvious—that the diversity and division in early Christianity cannot be taken as normative. The united church of tomorrow cannot be modeled after the divided church of the first century. The sooner we recognize that it was divided—although, of course, neither so deeply nor so fixedly as it is today—the sooner we can learn what the first age of the church, like each of the later ages, can teach us about the attainment of unity. For the first age of the church is, under one very important aspect, simply the first age of the church; that is, it is of a piece with all the later ages and shares in the character of the total history. Church history does not begin where the New Testament leaves off; it begins where the New Testament begins. The factors which during the long course of Christian history have operated to divide us and to keep us divided were operating

16

also in the Apostolic Age. That age can teach us out of its experience in resisting these forces of division, but is not itself the perfect example of unity. Only further and continued division can result from our accepting it as such.

A second and very closely related value in our recognizing that the primitive church was not "visibly" united is that we are thus enabled to give due heed to what can be called the ecumenical movement in early Christianity and to profit from it as we should. I am referring, of course, to the so-called Catholic movement, which is usually thought of as a late-second-century development, but whose beginnings can be easily discerned within the New Testament period itself, once we are set free from the illusion that the New Testament church was already united. Was the Catholic movement an effort to recover a lost unity? If so, we can afford perhaps to ignore it, or at least to give it scant attention as we also (like the early Catholics) push back to the lost original. But suppose there was no lost unity and that the Catholic movement represented the first large-scale effort to unite a divided Christendom. In that case, we must give it both attention and respect. It becomes the great prototype of our modern crusade for unity. We can profit from its mistakes; but we must not fail to recognize its successes. Since the movement had results solid, constructive, and decisively important for the whole subsequent history of the church, we must acknowledge and build on its achievements. We must not dismiss the measure of sound unity it achieved as being unimportant in comparison with the supposed perfect unity of an earlier period. The recognition that there had been no such earlier period invests the early Catholic movement with an interest and importance—yes, with an authority—which it deserves and which we must acknowledge if we are ever going really to achieve the unity it sought.

Finally, may I urge that the recognition of the divided character of early Christianity will have the value of forcing our attention beyond the church itself—whether Protestant, Catholic, or primitive—to the event which alone determined the fundamental character of the church and therefore was, and is, the ground of its unity. Now although it is true, as we have seen, that "under one very important aspect" the Apostolic Age was simply a period —albeit the first period—of church history, it is at least equally important for us to recognize that under another aspect the first age of the church is unique and has unique relevance. This is because it stands next to the event Jesus Christ, which does have authority and normative significance in the church in all the ages. In the early church's experience that event occurred in a different sense from any in which it may be said to occur in ours; and the records of that experience which the early church produced are an indispensable source for the recovery of the event in its original character and impact. This is the justification for the New Testament canon; and here is the undeniable and inalienable distinction of the early church.

But two additional considerations must be borne in mind if we are not to see this distinction in false perspective. The first is that it is the event which gives the Apostolic Age any significance it has; the importance does not reside in the age itself. The Apostolic Age is in its intrinsic character like every subsequent age. The recognition that it was not the age of the undivided church helps us to see this fact and to press back through the early church's experience to the ultimately normative reality itself. The second consideration is that the event was in its essence the coming of the Spirit and that this same Spirit was and is still the creative, constitutional, and animating principle of the church. The church is thus more than the consequence of the event; in its life the event continually recurs. The Spirit (in whose first coming the event consisted and in whose presence it

18

happens continually) belongs to the church as much in one century as in any other. The ground of the church's being, and therefore of its unity, is not something belonging simply to the church itself, but is the reality known in the beginning of the church's life as the event and in the center of its life as the Spirit, the one answering to the other as deep calleth unto deep. In this reality all the ages of the church participate, and by it they are judged. We participate as certainly as the first generation of Christians; they are judged as certainly as we.

It is with these earliest generations of Christians that we shall be principally concerned in this book. After considering the evidences of variety and division in the primitive church (in the following chapter), we shall seek to identify the principle of unity in its life—that is, the meaning of "event" and "Spirit" as they were received and understood. We shall then consider the efforts which the early church made toward the visible embodiment of this unity—what I have ventured to call the ecumenical movement in the early church. The final chapter will be devoted to an attempt to assess the relevance, the normative significance, of the primitive church's experience for the ecumenical movement of our own time.

DIVERSITY AND DIVISION
IN THE EARLY CHURCH

I<small>T WAS TO BE EXPECTED THAT CHRISTIANITY IN</small>
its earliest phase would be marked by considerable variety.[1]
Spreading from Palestine throughout the Mediterranean world
so rapidly that within twenty years Christian congregations were
to be found in many of the principal cities of the eastern prov-
inces, throughout Greece and Macedonia, and as far west as
Rome, its character was bound to be affected, in surface respects
at least, by the various environments from which the first Christians were drawn. It is by no means certain that even in Palestine Christianity was strictly of one type; [2] once it emerged from
Palestine, it was quite certain not to be.

This is the more obviously true because the spread was not
only rapid but also in considerable part undirected and uncon-
trolled. There is no evidence that the evangelization of the
Greco-Roman world went according to any "plan"—unless it
was God's plan. Although missionaries like Paul played an important part in the process of expansion, they were no more than

[1] It is obvious that an adequate discussion of the theme of this chapter
cannot be attempted here. The reader is referred to such histories of the
Apostolic Age as those of Weizäcker, McGiffert, J. Weiss, Lietzmann, Goguel,
and others, and also to such special studies as will be referred to in this
chapter in various connections.

[2] See p. 33.

carriers of a living Spirit, contagious as a flame; and we can be sure that at least some of the local churches in existence at the end of the first century had not been established by apostles or other prominent evangelists but had come, as it were, spontaneously into being because "two or three" Christian "laymen," recently come to a town or city, found one another or because a single such Christian shared his new life and faith with some of his neighbors. Under the conditions of such rapid growth over so wide and culturally diversified an area, we should not have expected uniformity in theology or practice. The surprising thing is that we find as much as we do, and that Christianity was recognizably itself wherever it was found. That under the circumstances it conquered the world, instead of being assimilated and destroyed by it, bears impressive witness to the vitality and integrity of the new movement. To a consideration of this vitality and integrity, which were also the early church's unity, we shall be turning in the following chapter.

An additional reason why one might have expected variety in the primitive church lies in the fact that the earliest Christians looked almost momentarily for the end of the present age. An important element in the preaching of the first evangelists was this prediction, with the accompanying warning that only Christ could save from the coming wrath. He was shortly to return; meantime it behooved all men everywhere to repent. The time was short—hardly long enough to permit the evangelists to bring the gospel within the hearing of all men, surely not long enough to organize churches and establish their practices on the basis of any uniform pattern. And why was such uniformity necessary or desirable anyhow in view of the Lord's early return, when all the orders of this world would be dissolved? Some kind of order would of course have been necessary from the start, and the various usages of the various congregations undoubtedly

21

shared many common features; [3] but would much store have been set by uniformity in detail? Although these are all a priori considerations, their force is really irresistible except for those who begin with another a priori, more dogmatic in character— namely, not only that Jesus foresaw the long future of the church and firmly and clearly laid down the lines of its development, but also (and this is the even more difficult part of the assumption) that his followers fully understood his plan and succeeded perfectly in accomplishing it.

But in asserting a wide range of variety in the primitive church we are not, of course, dependent upon a priori considerations alone. Our earliest literary sources fully support the assertion. The very existence of a New Testament with such diversified content bears strong witness. No critical reader of the New Testament can fail to be impressed by what E. F. Scott called "the varieties of New Testament religion." [4] Scott was thinking chiefly about what might be called the theology of the New Testament; and the point about variety can perhaps be most obviously made as regards ways of understanding and formulating the Christian message. Compare the Synoptic Gospels with John, or Matthew with Paul, or First Peter with Revelation, or James with Romans or Hebrews, or Hebrews and Romans with each other; indeed, compare any two books (or groups of books) by different authors, and you confront a much wider diversity of belief than can be found between almost any two of our modern denominations. And this diversity cannot be limited to belief. Dr. Frederick C. Grant clearly brings this out, as well as stressing the reality and depth of the theological differences themselves, when he writes:

[3] See pp. 84-87 for some account of these significant common features.
[4] In a book published under that title (New York: Chas. Scribner's Sons, 1943).

[The diversity] is not limited to choice of language, as if the New Testament writers all meant the same thing but selected different words for saying it. The diversity involves some of the basic ideas of New Testament theology; the religious attitude, ethos, and approach of quite different groups; and also a variety in practice, in organization, and in types of religious activity, which the studies of the past generation have made so clearly evident that no fair-minded student can ignore them. Unless he is obsessed by a preconceived theory, ecclesiastical or other, he will be compelled to reckon with this genuine and far-reaching diversity in the religion of the New Testament.[5]

As a matter of fact, we can be sure that the religion of the early church was even more diversified than the religion of the New Testament, because the New Testament represents a selection from among documents in the interest of unity, and documents representing certain extremes have been excluded. Moreover, it is likely that some strains in primitive Christianity were not significant enough to produce documents at all or for some other reason did not do so. Both Grant and Scott would insist as strongly upon the unity of early Christianity as upon its variety. But the real nature of this unity cannot be seen until the diversity is fully taken into account; nor, indeed, can its strength be truly estimated. For it was a unity strong enough not only to tolerate a wide variety of belief and practice, but also, as we shall see a little later, to bear the strains of deep division between important leaders and large groups of Christians.

I

We have sometimes been led to underestimate the extent of diversity in the early church by the very factor that has been most responsible for enabling us to see and acknowledge the

---

[5] *An Introduction to New Testament Thought* (New York and Nashville: Abingdon Press, 1950), p. 30. Used by permission of the publishers.

existence of the diversity itself—namely, our recognition of the dynamic character of primitive Christianity. The habit of looking at the New Testament as the record of a developing community life (rather than as a mere description of a static thing) represents one of the great benefits that biblical historical study of the last century or so has conferred. We have come to see that our picture of primitive Christianity is a "moving picture" (no true picture of history, of course, can be anything else). We have thus grown accustomed to thinking of early Acts, of Paul, of Mark, of John, as reflecting successive stages in the development of early Christian life and thought. This is in itself pure gain; but there is a certain danger in it, the danger of supposing that the development was proceeding in orderly sequence consistently "across the board," the same new stage displacing the old, every time and everywhere. But nothing is clearer than that this was not true. "Paulinism" was not a stage in the development of Christianity in every place; nor even where it existed did it always give place to "Johanninism." More "primitive" views or practices persisted in one community long after more "advanced" ideas and usages had been adopted by another. In a word, the variety of the New Testament cannot be interpreted as representing merely a variety in time—that is, a diversity as between chronological periods; it is also a variety in place. And who will say that there was not sometimes variety among different communities in the same time and place? [6] Modern studies that emphasize the geographical element in the story of the early church have provided a necessary corrective to the earlier, more simple, chronological interpretation, and they should keep us

[6] This possibility is often involved in discussions of the destination of the Epistle to the Hebrews, for example. Some students of the epistle claim that it was written to a particular community, or to several particular communities, in Rome.

from forgetting the persistent, and often deepening, character of the diversities among the early communities.[7]

These same studies have put us on guard against making generalizations about the prevalence of a particular Christian belief or practice in a given period because we have found an instance or two of it in the canonical or other early documents. This peril is especially hard to avoid because of our natural desire, on the one hand, to achieve as general a conception as possible of early Christianity, and because of the paucity of our source materials, on the other. It is hard to keep a "voice" in one place from filling the "silence" somewhere else. It is hard not to supply what we are not told about one period or region from what we are told about another; or to refrain from putting together a fragmentary account of practices in one church and a similarly partial account of the usages in another in order to make a complete picture of what went on in both. Or, again, we may easily decide that an account of an early Christian usage in one place is "partial" only because, if taken as complete, it cannot be easily harmonized with another account of the same practice in another place.

We may conclude, for example, that Justin Martyr's description of a Roman church service around A.D. 150, Pliny's account of the services of the church in Bithynia-Pontus a generation earlier, and Paul's description of what went on in the services at Corinth are all partial accounts of the same thing.[8] Justin Martyr does

---

[7] Among such studies are R. A. Aytoun, *City Centres of Early Christianity* (London: Hodder & Stoughton, 1915) ; K. Lake, *Landmarks in the History of Early Christianity* (New York: The Macmillan Co., 1922) ; B. H. Streeter, *The Four Gospels* (New York: The Macmillan Co., 1925) and *The Primitive Church* (New York: The Macmillan Co., 1929) . For a brief summary of the history of Christianity in each of the major centers of early Christian life, see M. H. Shepherd, Jr., "The History of the Early Church: The Post-Apostolic Age," *The Interpreter's Bible* (New York and Nashville: Abingdon Press) , VII, 214-27.

[8] Justin *Apology* I. 67; Pliny *Letters* X. 96; I Cor. 11-14.

not mention any music or singing in what would appear to be a full outline of the Roman service in this period; but Pliny's letter refers to singing as an important part of the service in Bithynia-Pontus; and references in Paul's letters, Revelation,[9] and elsewhere indicate that also at other times and places music was a feature of early Christian worship. Obviously, therefore (we are likely to argue), Justin has omitted this item from his description. Perhaps he has; but can we be sure? So far as the documentary evidence goes, it is not clear that the Roman service in this period included music.[10] On the other hand, Pliny and Paul give no indication that scripture reading was an element in common worship, whereas Justin ascribes the greatest importance to reading "from the memoirs of the apostles or the writings of the prophets." Is this discrepancy to be explained as owing to omissions by Pliny and Paul? Perhaps so; their accounts do not need to be taken as complete. But is it not possible that a real difference in practice is indicated? One notes in this connection that Paul not only makes no reference to the reading of scripture—this lack is particularly striking in I Cor. 14:26—but does not include reading among the spiritual gifts. It is also noteworthy in this connection that Pliny, although he clearly took pains to find out exactly what happened in the Christians' meetings, apparently does not know of any connection of Christianity

[9] I Cor. 14:26; Col. 3:16; Rev. 5:9 ff.; *et passim*. These references to music are unmistakable, but many would dispute that Pliny's words *carmenque Christo quasi deo dicere secum invicem* refer to singing.

[10] Since the Roman service described by Justin so clearly follows the synagogue pattern, it is interesting to note that, according to some students, the synagogues of the New Testament period did not include the singing of psalms in their services (see W. Bauer, *Der Wortgottesdienst der ältesten Christen* [Tübingen: J. C. B. Mohr, 1930], pp. 21-22). H. Lietzmann (*The Beginnings of the Christian Church* [New York: Chas. Scribner's Sons, 1937], pp. 195-96) argues that this may not have been true of the Hellenistic synagogues, but there seems to be no assurance of this.

with Judaism—a connection which a reading of the Jewish Scriptures in their services would have made conspicuous, even (one might suppose) inescapable.[11]

All our sources agree that the Lord's Supper (although we must allow for more than one form) [12] was an essential and constant element in worship. Justin quite clearly, and Paul by implication, knows the Supper as the central element in one inclusive service of worship. One might gather from Paul (I Cor. 11:20) that the Supper provided the framework of the entire service. Pliny, however, explicitly declares that the Christians, after their first service of praise and dedication, dispersed and met again later for the service of the Eucharist (and probably also the Agape). If a generalization has to be made, I should regard the single service as more probable; [13] but why do we need to make a generalization? Why not recognize that two practices may have prevailed at different times or at different places?

Professor Cullmann, after citing the Justin account and insisting that in the service described there "we are not dealing with a later development, for . . . the Eucharist and the other elements of worship, above all the proclamation of the Word, are bound up together . . . from the beginning," goes on to say:

A change has taken place, however, by the time of Justin in another connection. . . . We find that the free expressions of the Spirit such

[11] It is argued by some that the use of the Decalogue is indicated by Pliny's statement that the Christians "bound themselves by an oath . . . not to commit theft or robbery or adultery, not to break their word, and not to deny a trust when demanded." But the indications are not clear, and in any case no reading of scripture is necessarily involved.

[12] See, e.g., E. Lohmeyer, "Das Abendmahl in der Urgemeinde," *Journal of Biblical Literature,* LVI (1937), pp. 217-52.

[13] See O. Cullmann, *Early Christian Worship* (London: S.C.M. Press, 1953), pp. 26-32. The union of the two elements seems to be indicated in Acts 2:42 and 20:7-11; but see Acts 5:42 and 2:46, where the two elements are spoken of separately.

as prophesying, speaking with tongues, and interpretation of tongues
have disappeared. What remains, apart from the Eucharist, appears
now, but only now in this later form, as an adaptation of the synagogue service.[14]

I hesitate to take issue with such a scholar as Cullmann; but I
wonder how he knows that this character of the Roman service
(that is, a synagogue service with the addition of the Eucharist)
belongs only to a "later form." Is there any indication at all that
the Roman service had ever been different? Nothing in First
Clement or First Peter or Hebrews points in any other direction.
And, if anything, Paul's Letter to the Romans rather confirms
Justin. Paul says he is coming to impart a "spiritual gift" as
though to suggest that the Roman church, whatever its excel-
lences, was deficient in ecstatic experience; and in his discussion
(12:3-8) of the gifts and functions exemplified in the life of the
church, he avoids any mention of the gifts that were the center
of attention in I Cor. 11–14—namely, the gifts of tongues and
interpretation. The supposition that Roman worship was from
the start more orderly and sober than that in Paul's churches (or
at least in some of them, because we have no right to assume
that Corinth was altogether typical even of Paul's congregations)
—this supposition is in line with our best surmise about the
origins of the Roman church, which is that it originated among
converted members of the Jewish community in Rome. The more
"Jewish" worship in Rome in A.D. 150 does not represent a
development of the more Hellenistic worship in Corinth in A.D.

50. Modes of worship in the Christian churches—Jewish, proselyte, pagan in background, and in various mixtures—were diversified from the start, although, of course, they shared certain
common and distinctive characteristics.

[14] *Op. cit.,* p. 30.

These illustrations have all been taken from the worship of the early church, but the same kind of picture appears when we consider its theology and its polity.[15] We have already noted that in theology not only was there constant change in the way the new empirical fact of Christ was understood and interpreted, but these changes were following more than one line of development; and, we may be sure, even the changes in a single line were not proceeding at the same rate everywhere. The writer to the Hebrews, for example, is in some respects a "contemporary" of Paul and in others of the Fourth Gospel. The community for which he speaks (and to some extent he must speak for a community) was quite "advanced" in some of its theology and almost "primitive" in other parts. The theology of most communities, we may believe, was similarly mixed and indeterminate. There was no conformity to a stereotype, if only because no stereotype had been established.

When we turn to polity, we find evidence of the same fluidity, the same lack of consistency. Did the apostles and other early evangelists have definite views as to how the churches they established should be organized? To what extent did these views differ? How is the relation between the "prophets and teachers" and the "bishops and deacons" to be thought of? Did every church have one type of church officer or the other—either the

[15] On polity see, e.g., O. Linton, *Das Problem der Urkirche in der neueren Foschung* (Uppsala: Lundequistska, 1932); B. H. Streeter, *The Primitive Church;* W. D. Davies, *A Normative Pattern of Church Life in the New Testament: Fact or Fancy?* (London: James Clarke & Co., 1950). A number of additional titles are indicated in Chapter V (especially footnote 18). On theological belief, see any good study of New Testament theology (e.g., H. J. Holtzmann, Beyschlag, Bultmann, etc.) and the works of Grant and Scott mentioned earlier in this chapter. W. Bauer, *Rechtgläubigkeit und Ketzerei im ältesten Christentum* (Tübingen: J. C. B. Mohr, 1934) is concerned chiefly with the second century, but it throws great light upon the theological diversity of the first.

"charismatic" or the "institutional"—or did the two types coexist in the same church? How long did the Pauline churches depend on a "charismatic" leadership? Did they ever entirely depend on it? Or can we generalize about the organization of even the Pauline churches? How, when, and where did the bishops (apparently originally identical with elders) come to be distinguished from the elders? Where and when did monepiscopacy arise, and by what stages did it establish itself among the churches? These are all questions to which no clear answer can be given—almost certainly because, in respect to this matter of organization and government, as in every other respect, the early churches reflected the diversities of their several backgrounds, their several origins, and their several histories.[16]

So much for the diversity of primitive Christianity. But were there also conflict and division?

II

The uncritical student of the New Testament and of Christian origins, even if he is ready to acknowledge some variety, is likely to think of Christianity in the primitive period as free not only from schism but also from any threat of it, as actually embodying "the unity of the Spirit in the bond of peace." Among the several considerations mentioned in the preceding chapter as helping to account for the prevalence of this impression is the fact that the New Testament itself from time to time lays stress upon the unity of the church. Now much the most influential book of the New Testament in this respect is the book of Acts. This book is the only canonical, indeed the only early, history we have of the Apostolic Age; no wonder our impressions of that age are

[16] For evidences of significant agreements and similarities in all these respects see pp. 63-129.

so largely derived from it. But the very fact that Acts stands alone as our only early history of the primitive church should put us on guard against too quick and easy an acceptance of its statements. All histories are necessarily incomplete, selective, and somewhat tendentious, and this is especially true of ancient histories; and the accidental fact that we are not able to prove the inaccuracy of a particular historian by referring to a parallel account must not be permitted to create a presumption of accuracy. Of course, it is equally true that such a fact does not justify us in presuming inaccuracies; it simply challenges us to exercise caution and critical care.

Now there are at least two reasons for questioning the reliability of Acts as to the extent of unity and division in the early church. The first of these is the fact that the narrative in Acts manifestly covers only a part of the story of the expansion of Christianity in the Apostolic Age. Although the author has been understood to promise (Acts 1:8) that he will tell us of the extension of the movement from Jerusalem in all directions to the uttermost parts of the world, he actually follows only one line of that expansion, the line which led through Syria to Asia Minor and the Greek peninsula. It might be argued that this was the only extra-Palestinian area into which Christianity actually expanded in the first century, if there were not clear evidence that the movement reached Rome and some evidence that it had also come to Alexandria. Even Acts seems to hint (18:24-25) that Alexandria had been reached, just as it confirms (28:14-15) the indubitable witness of Paul himself (in Romans) that the church was already to be found in Rome. But it tells us nothing whatever as to when or how either of these churches had been established and gives no hint as to the kind of church it was. One is bound to wonder also about the movement of Christianity toward the East. The relations of Palestine with the Jews of Babylonia were close, and one would have expected a very early entrance of Christian missionaries into that region. Paul speaks of a trip of his own into "Arabia" (the territory just east of Damascus), but Acts does not speak of this or indeed of any eastward thrust. But such a thrust must have occurred quite early, surely long before the book of Acts, on any theory of its date, was written. Later legend, of course, supplies all that is lacking; according to the third-century Acts of Thomas the whole world was divided by lot among the twelve apostles, Thomas himself going to India and the others to their several fields. But the efflorescence of legend only calls attention to the obvious gaps in the only authentic narrative we have for the earliest period. The book of Acts is not an adequate guide to the extent of diversity in the primitive church, because it confines its attention to only a part of the field.

But there is another reason for caution. The writer of Acts has an interest in accenting the note of unity in the early church and in discounting or ignoring evidences of division. Whether we date Acts toward the end of the first century or fairly early in the second, it clearly reflects the beginnings of the Catholic movement, the movement toward consolidation which dominates second-century Christianity. Like us, and for much the same reason, the author looks back nostalgically to the ideal unity of the primitive church. As he sees it, the apostles or "the apostles and elders," settled in Jerusalem, the actual and symbolic center of Israel, governed from that same center the new Israel, overseeing its expansion and regulating its life. Sharp differences of opinion or practice occasionally occur among the churches, but such disputes are quickly and authoritatively settled. Paul works with, because loyally under, the apostles. He appoints "elders . . . in every church" he founds, who are presumably subject to him just as he is subject to Jerusalem. But even Acts itself has difficulty in making this irenic picture of the early church really plausible and consistent, and the letters of Paul all but demolish it.

Not only can a question be raised as to the extent and kind of authority the Jerusalem leaders exercised in the expanding church, but there is also ground for doubt that the process of expansion even began from that one center. Ernst Lohmeyer [17] has developed a strong case for the view that Galilee was also a center of Christianity in the most primitive—that is, the Palestinian—period. The Gospel story would have led one to expect that this would be true, and, as Lohmeyer shows, indications are not lacking that it was. The variant traditions in Mark-Matthew and Luke-Acts-John as to the place of the resurrection appearances (and therefore, by clear implication, the place where the church really began) point in this direction. There are signs that Galilee not only "competed" with Jerusalem but represented a somewhat different type of Christianity. If so, the failure of Acts to refer to any developments in Galilee (where Jesus' ministry had largely taken place and where it must have left some fruit) can be understood.

The fact of the matter is that the data of Acts reflect much more clearly and surely the absence of a desired unity in the writer's own period than the presence of that unity in an earlier time. It is much more certain that the churches and church leaders toward the end of the century were not "of one accord" than that the author of Acts had any really sound reason for saying, as he often does, that the early apostles and their associates were. We may well doubt that Paul actually spoke to

[17] *Galiläa und Jerusalem* (Göttingen: Vandenhoeck & Rupprecht, 1936); see also F. C. Grant, *The Earliest Gospel* (New York and Nashville: Abingdon Press, 1943), pp. 125-47.

the Ephesian elders at Miletus in the way recorded in Acts 20:
18-35, predicting that "wolves" would come in, "not sparing
the flock," and that among the Christians themselves would arise
men "speaking perverse things" and drawing "away the disciples
after them"; but we can be sure that when Acts was being
written, the prediction had been fulfilled—and not only at
Ephesus but widely among the churches. In the same way, as
we have seen,[18] the strong affirmation in Ephesians of the unity
of the church is to be understood, at least in part, as a confession
of the lack of it. Otherwise the affirmation and implicit exhortation would not be needed. Similarly, the great prayer ascribed to
Jesus in John 17, "that they may all be one," is the more poignant
for revealing, as it does, that at the end of the century, when
the Fourth Gospel was written, his followers were still divided.
And the rebuke by Jesus (Mark 9:38; Luke 9:49) of the disciples who had forbidden an exorcist to cast out demons in
Christ's name because he had not "followed" with them—must
not this, at least in part, be understood as a rebuke in that same
name of the jealousies and divisions in the apostolic church? The
same thing can be said about Jesus' reproof of the ambitiousness
of two of his disciples who wanted to have chief places in the
kingdom.

That such jealousies and divisions existed, there is quite enough
more positive evidence to show. In his letter to the Philippians
(1:15-18) Paul refers to those who are preaching Christ "from
envy and rivalry, . . . out of partisanship, not sincerely but thinking to afflict [him] in [his] imprisonment." (How shameful a
motive! And yet does not the history of the church, and indeed
what we find in our own hearts, make it credible?) The same
apostle is constantly urging his readers to be "of one mind"
(II Cor. 13:11; Phil. 2:2) or reminding them that they are "one

[18] See p. 14.

in Christ" (Gal. 3:28). Such exhortations tell us quite as much about the realities of church life as they do about Paul's ideal for it.

A considerable part of First Corinthians is devoted to the disturbing factions in Corinth. One gathers that the church there was divided along a number of lines (the divided church of history might be found there in microcosm). Apparently the divisions were partly social in origin, the richer withdrawing from the poorer (11:22-23); the racial issue may have been involved; intellectual differences were partly responsible, as some members of the church made pretensions to a "wisdom" which others could not, or would not, claim; differences of opinion about moral conduct and probably some theological differences also had their effect; and, most conspicuous of all, of course, were exclusive loyalties to various church leaders. Just how these lines of division were related to one another—how far they coincided and to what extent they cut across one another, making parties within parties—we are not told. But there can be no doubt that serious factions divided the church at Corinth; and the letter of the church at Rome to the church at Corinth (First Clement), written, it is usually held, about A.D. 96, reveals that this situation still existed in Corinth or had recurred.

It must be recognized, of course, that Paul in First Corinthians is concerned with divisions in a church—that is, in one congregation—not with divisions in the church generally or among the churches. But it is unlikely that the factions at Corinth were entirely local. Of the three men around whom parties had formed,[19] Paul and Peter at least were universally recognized

---

[19] I am inclined to agree with J. Weiss that the apparent reference to a party of Christ ("I am of Christ") in I Cor. 1:12 represents a later interpolation. See J. Weiss, *A History of Primitive Christianity* (New York: Wilson-Erickson, Inc., 1937), I, 340; also his commentary on First Corinthians, pp. 15-18.

leaders of the church; little is known of Apollos, but he too may well have become influential in a wide circle of congregations (compare I Cor. 16:12 and Acts 18:24-28). But whatever may be said about Apollos, we can scarcely doubt that the parties of Peter and Paul reflected in some measure a conflict in the church at large. And this is particularly true because we know that such a conflict was then going on—a conflict in which they were principal figures and which had deeply divided the churches, both within themselves and from one another.

III

This conflict had begun, or at any rate the ground for it had been laid, when the first non-Jew accepted the new faith. We do not know when this occurred; but it was certainly quite early, perhaps within a year or two of Jesus' crucifixion in A.D. 29 or 30. In any case, by A.D. 35 or so there were flourishing Christian churches in cities as far from Jerusalem as Damascus and Antioch; and it is likely that these churches from the very beginning were, at least in considerable part, Gentile in constituency. Shortly afterward Paul, conceiving of himself as the apostle to the Gentiles, carried the gospel further west, possibly into Cilicia, certainly into Galatia, Asia, Macedonia, and Greece; and there can be no possible doubt that the churches he established were largely, perhaps sometimes exclusively, made up of non-Jews.

Now among all the diverse nations and cultures that belonged to the "one world" Rome had forged, none was so distinctive as Judaism. In the course of its stubborn fight over several centuries against assimilation, it had developed cultural characteristics and mores which set it off, not only from each of the other nations, but also from all these nations together, as the very term "Gentiles" ("nations") indicates. Nonassociation with Gen-

tiles, or at most very limited association, was one of the primary
tenets of Judaism. When, therefore, large numbers of non-Jews
were received directly out of paganism into what had been
originally a society of Jews, the most serious problems were
created, especially for the members of the older Jewish community. Should not these new converts (they would very naturally
argue) accept the obligations along with the privileges of
Judaism? How could they share in Christ, the fulfillment of the
law and the prophets, unless they observed the law and the
prophets themselves? How could one belong to the new covenant
who did not first, or also, belong to the old? Jesus and his disciples, even Paul, were Jews, and the original communities were
Jewish communities—it could not have been otherwise, for
Christianity is the true Israel—but how could one belong to
the true Israel who did not belong to Israel at all? Such questions were very natural ones; and to those who asked them the
admission of Gentiles to the church, without the requirement of
circumcision and submission to the Jewish law, would have
seemed an intolerable anomaly. Many were not content merely
to hold such views but became active propagandists for the Jewish
position in the Gentile churches (at least among the churches in
Paul's area). We hear of them in Galatia, in Philippi, and, almost certainly, in Corinth.[20] Whether these so-called Judaizers
were official representatives of some group or groups or were
"on their own," we do not know. We do know not only that
they were active among Paul's converts but also that they were
influential in raising doubts as to both the truth of his doctrine
and the validity of his authority.

To this challenge Paul responded with an almost savage
ferocity. Not only was an important element in his message im-

[20] See, e.g., Gal. 1:6-9, 5:12; Phil. 3:2-6; II Cor. 12:12-21.

plicated in this issue of whether Gentiles needed to observe the Jewish law, but also more personal and concrete considerations were involved, indeed nothing less than his own calling as an apostle and the very existence of his churches. For the latter he fought as a mother fights for her young. The paragraph in Philippians to which I have referred, as well as II Cor. 10–13, and the whole of Galatians, will reveal how bitter the battle was. The struggle may have been more or less continuous throughout Paul's career as an apostle, building up to a climax near its close, a climax reflected in the passages I have just cited, in two anxious trips to Jerusalem, and probably also in the tragic frustration in which his hopes for further evangelistic work in Rome and Spain finally ended; so I would understand the indications of our meager sources.[21] Others would regard the fight as less continuous but as consisting in recurring bitter engagements. But however we reconstruct the chronology of this struggle, there can be no doubt both of the fact of it and of its persistence and bitterness. Nor can we think of it merely as a battle among individuals, Paul and perhaps Barnabas and a few others on one side and a dozen or so unnamed Jews on the other; these were only the leaders of, and spokesmen for, two large parties in the church, and all the deep diversities between Jewish and Gentile culture were involved.

Paul tells us (Gal. 2:1-10) that at a crucial point in the great conflict he went to Jerusalem to consult with those who were regarded as the leaders there and that he laid before them the gospel he was preaching among the Gentiles. At this conference the position of Paul as to the freedom of the Gentiles from the requirements of the Jewish ceremonial law was apparently fully

[21] This reconstruction I have tried to justify in my *Chapters in a Life of Paul* (New York and Nashville: Abingdon Press, 1950).

validated. Titus, a Greek, who had accompanied Paul on his journey, was not forced to be circumcised; that is (presumably), the leaders did not insist that he should be. On the contrary, they recognized that circumcision was not properly to be asked of Gentiles and that Paul and Barnabas had been proceeding along right lines, just as Peter, working among Jews, had been right in taking circumcision for granted. "When they perceived," Paul writes, "the grace that was given to me, James and Cephas and John, who were reputed to be pillars, gave to me and Barnabas the right hand of fellowship, that we should go to the Gentiles and they to the circumcised." This action, Paul, Barnabas, and the three Jerusalem leaders probably hoped, would end the struggle. Events proved that it did not. It did not because the solution proposed called for a divided church; and this neither Paul nor the Judaizers were prepared to accept.

That division was implied in the Jerusalem formula may not have been seen at first by Paul, or by Peter, or even at the time by James, but it appeared soon afterward. In a paragraph which follows immediately on his account of the conference, Paul recounts (Gal. 2:11 ff.) an occurrence in Antioch that made this meaning of the Jerusalem action, at least as James now understood it, unmistakable. Jews and Gentiles in the Antioch church had been accustomed to share together in the common meal (with which no doubt the Eucharist was closely associated). Peter as well as Paul, both visiting the church at the time, joined in this common celebration. But when "certain men came from James," Peter "drew back and separated himself, fearing the circumcision party"; and he was joined by "the rest of the Jews." In other words, it now appeared that James had agreed to the admission of Gentiles to the church without circumcision only with the understanding that there should be in effect two separate churches, not in communion with each other, a Gentile church and a Jewish church. Neither Paul nor his Judaizing opponents were willing to accept such a compromise. The battle, therefore, continued—probably to the very end of Paul's career.

This chapter may appropriately close with the recognition that Paul was fighting not only for the freedom of the Gentiles from the law but also for the unity of the church. Must not this be the meaning of the strange statement that he went to consult the Jerusalem leaders "lest somehow [he] should be running or had run in vain" (Gal. 2:2)? He cannot mean that he regards the truth of his gospel as dependent upon the approval of the "pillars" or that he is acknowledging their authority to pass on his apostleship. But he must mean more than that he fears his opponents may seriously interfere with his work unless they are checked. What can be expressed here if not Paul's deep concern that the church shall be one? The church indeed *must* be one; and yet it was not. He suffered the same pains of the divided body we also suffer. The Judaizers had an easier solution; they had only to exclude the Gentiles in order to have one church. In the same way no doubt there were Gentile Christians who felt no need of fellowship with Jews.[22] But Paul, who fought for the freedom of the Gentiles, would not have been able to exclude the Jews; the church must be recognized as fully including both. The fight of Paul was a fight for ecumenicity, but it divided the

[22] See A. C. McGiffert, *The God of the Early Christians* (New York: Chas. Scribner's Sons, 1924), for evidence of the existence of a purely Gentile Christianity. Such a Christianity may be thought of as providing the background of the second-century Marcion and perhaps of the bulk of his followers. See also in this connection W. Bauer, *Rechtgläubigkeit und Ketzerei im ältesten Christentum* (Tübingen: J. C. B. Mohr, 1934).

church; or, rather, it brought into the open and made manifest a division which already lay deep in its life.[23]

---

[23] This breach Paul hoped might be healed by the offering he undertook at the "pillars'" suggestion (Gal. 2:10). (Does the use of the strange expression in Rom. 15:28, "sealed to them this fruit" [σφραγισάμενος αὐτοῖς τὸν καρπὸν τοῦτον], have anything to do with this purpose?) What seems to have happened in Jerusalem when he went to deliver it (if we may judge from the Acts account, making due allowance for its theory of early Christian concord and unity) does not reassure us that this purpose was actually fulfilled or that the offering was cordially received (εὐπρόσδεκτος, Rom. 15:31). It is possible that the breach was never healed; and that it ceased to raise an acute issue only because Palestinian and specifically Jewish Christianity itself, especially after the revolt of A.D. 66-70, became relatively unimportant, an eddy which the great stream flowed past.

A new emphasis upon the reality and depth of the differences between Pauline and Palestinian Christianity has been placed by S. G. F. Brandon in *The Fall of Jerusalem and the Christian Church* (London: Society for Promoting Christian Knowledge, 1951), especially in pp. 31-87. Not all Brandon's arguments in these pages, or in the book as a whole, are convincing; but they add up to a strong case for real division in the early church, as well as being worthy of attention for other reasons.

THE SHARED LIFE

MORE THAN ONCE IN THE PRECEDING chapter reference was made to the unity of the primitive church; and if the picture of early Christianity is to be truly drawn, the reality of this unity must be stressed even more heavily than the variety—not to say disparity and division—we have been emphasizing thus far. If what we have observed about the early church up to this point were the whole story, the question would inevitably arise, "Can we speak of the 'early church' at all? Have we anything more than early churches?" The truth of the matter is, however, that the distinctiveness of the church as over against the world (both Jewish and pagan) was in the earliest period much more striking than were any diversities within the church itself. Christianity, wherever it was found, was a recognizable cultural phenomenon; and, moreover, every Christian group (with the possible exception of some of the more extreme Jewish congregations) was deeply aware of its own identity within a movement that included all the rest.

This fact of unity was not without its visible manifestations, despite all that was said in the previous chapter. There were, to be sure, diversities in the ways churches were governed; but the variations can be reduced to a few general types of polity, and even these types cannot be kept entirely separate or distinct.

42

There was no one over-all organization and no central control, as we have seen; but Jerusalem (until its destruction) seems to have enjoyed a certain pre-eminence and to have exerted a certain moderating, and therefore unifying, influence. We have also observed considerable variety in worship; but the Lord's Supper (though in different forms) seems to have been a common and constant feature, and baptism was from the start, or quickly came to be, the universal rite of initiation. These and other common elements of worship and polity we shall have occasion to consider briefly again in a later chapter. It is clear, however, that they are the consequences, or concomitants, of a deeper identity.

This deeper identity of the churches, and therefore this deeper unity of the church, had a double character and ground. It had an empirical basis in a shared life and a more ideational basis in a shared faith. This life and faith may seem to, and to an extent do, answer to the two realities mentioned near the close of the Introduction as being the ultimately normative realities in Christianity, the Spirit and the event: the distinctive *life* of the early community consisting in the realized presence of the Spirit, and its distinctive faith in the recognized meaning of the event. But such an analysis is only approximately true; for just as event and Spirit cannot be separated from each other, so Christian faith and life cannot be separated from either. The primitive church's *life* involved not only a common participation in the Spirit but also a common memory of the event; and the primitive church's recognition of the meaning of the event—that is, its *faith*—was possible only within the living community of the Spirit. Still, just as the event, which is the coming of the Spirit, can be distinguished, for purposes of discussion at least, from the church, which is the people of the Spirit, so we can distinguish between the faith and the life of the early church itself. There is a difference in order, however. The event must be thought of as preceding, and providing the ground for, the distinctive life of the community; but the *recognized significance* of the event, which is the faith, must be thought of as following upon, and finding its ground in, that same life. Therefore, we consider now the unifying life of the early church before turning, in the next chapter, to the common faith.[1]

I

At the outset we must make an attempt to realize the very great importance of the primitive church for both the Christian believer and the student of Christian origins. I do not mean the importance of the primitive *idea* of the church and of the various early conceptions of its nature and meaning—this we shall be at least touching on in a later chapter. Rather, I mean the importance—a far greater importance—of the early church itself as an existential fact. I say we must *make an attempt* to realize this importance, because apparently only by the exertion of a genuine effort are we able to recognize how completely primitive Christianity is identical with the early church and how dependent on it we are for any knowledge we can have of the event of Christ, what it was and what it accomplished. We are likely to think—or, better perhaps, to feel vaguely—that we have contact with the event in other ways and that there is "more to

[1] It will be recognized that I am using the term "faith" in only one of several possible senses. The word often means a personal response of trust, of self-abnegating surrender, in which alone the love of God in Christ can be known. So defined, "faith" would be an element in what we are calling the Christian "life"; that is, it would be an element in the empirical ground of "faith" in the sense in which the term is being used in the present discussion. In this latter sense, "faith" refers to the way in which the early church understood and interpreted the event which was the source and norm of its life.

Christianity" than the church. But what is this "more," and what are these "other ways"? Is it not obvious, when one reflects on it, that the sole residuum of the event was the church? The only difference between the world as it was just after the event and the world as it had been just before is that the church was now in existence. A new kind of human community had emerged; a new society had come into being. There was absolutely nothing besides. This new community held and prized vivid memories of the event in which it had begun. It had a new faith; that is, it saw the nature of the world and of God in a new light. It found in its own life the grounds—indeed, anticipatory fulfillments— of a magnificent hope. But the memory, the faith, and the hope were all its own; they had neither existence nor ground outside the community. Only the church really existed. Except for the church the event had not occurred.

This statement can be made because of two principal facts. The first of them is the historical insignificance of the career of Jesus of Nazareth in every other connection. It may be argued that this career was an event in Jewish history. In one sense it obviously was—that is, in the simple sense that it actually happened and happened within Palestinian Jewish society. But the Jewish nation, however understandably and for whatever reason, rejected him; and though it may be claimed that if they had given more heed to him, later events might have been different, it can hardly be contended that his career had to do in any more positive sense with the fate that was so soon to overtake them. It is held by some,[2] to be sure, that Jesus sought to exert

[2] As, for example, by V. G. Simkhovitch, *Toward the Understanding of Jesus* (New York: The Macmillan Co., 1921), and by C. J. Cadoux, *The Historic Mission of Jesus* (London: Lutterworth Press, 1941).

45

a political influence; but, even if so, there is no evidence that he succeeded in affecting the policies of the nation's leaders or, in any important way, the political opinions of its people. It may be argued also that if the Christian church had not come into existence as a distinct community—that is, if the followers of Jesus had not in effect separated themselves from Judaism by making messianic claims for Jesus and by disregarding, in his name, the requirements of the law—Jesus would have been remembered by his people as a great prophetic teacher and his words would have become an important element in the tradition of Judaism. But this is dubious and in any case irrelevant, since we are concerned with what actually occurred. The fact that Josephus' great work on Jewish history, the *Antiquities of the Jews,* contains only a few sentences about Jesus,[3] and some at least of these are of doubtful authenticity—this fact, if anything, exaggerates Jesus' own importance in Jewish history, since it is undoubtedly the existence of the church which led Josephus to mention him at all (if indeed he did). As for Greco-Roman history, it is even more clear that the career of Jesus, simply as such, had no significance. The meager references to it in Pliny, Tacitus, and (possibly) Suetonius are manifestly prompted solely by the activities and the growing importance of the church in the second century.[4] In a word, except for its connection with the church, the event of Jesus of Nazareth was hardly an event at all.

This last sentence suggests the second principal fact: namely, that the event to which the early church looked back was by definition an event that it alone could know; for this event occurred only within its life. We have seen that we are bound to

[3] 18. 3. 3; 20. 9. 1.

[4] Pliny *Letters* X. 96-97; Tacitus *Annals* XV. 44; Suetonius *Claudius* 25.

think of the event as having a certain precedence to the church, since it was through the event that the church came into being; but this precedence must not be understood as involving at any stage a merely chronological antecedence. It would be a great mistake to suppose that the event first occurred, and then the community came into existence. On the contrary, the occurrence of the event and the rise of the community proceeded together. As Jesus' ministry began, a group of disciples began to form about him; as the ministry continued, their community was presumably deepened and widened; his terrible death, while it shook their community to its foundations and tested it as with fire, also had the effect of bringing to poignant realization all he had meant to them; with his resurrection what we know as the early church came fully into being. But the church was obviously not a sudden emergent from an event already in the past. It had been gradually coming into being as the event developed, and indeed the event itself is inconceivable apart from it. The career of Jesus of Nazareth, simply as a human career, was, for all its intrinsic greatness, a relatively unimportant incident in Jewish history. The event of Jesus Christ the Lord was historically the important thing; and this event happened only in the life of the church.

This is most obviously true of the Resurrection, because in that connection our sources themselves make the point all but explicit; it was only to his disciples that he "presented himself alive after his passion." [5] But it is equally true of the Crucifixion and the teaching—indeed of the whole person and career of Jesus—for it was only as these were received and understood by his disciples that they became a part of the event. For the event

[5] I do not regard Paul as an exception here. See my *Chapters in a Life of Paul* (New York and Nashville: Abingdon Press, 1950), pp. 123-27.

was by definition a revealing event; and about such an event it must be recognized not only that one cannot see or bear witness to it unless one receives the revelation, but also that only in the experience of those who receive the revelation can the revealing event be said to occur at all. To be sure, the Crucifixion took place "under Pontius Pilate"; and it is not an accident that such a historical datum is in the creed, for the fact of the Crucifixion, as of the whole career of Jesus, was a fact in no sense or degree less objective than other facts of nature and history, and it is important that it be recognized as such. But the revelatory meaning of that fact was known only within the church; and that meaning was an integral part of the event itself. Thus, the event as such happened only there; it was remembered only there and can be found only there.

But not only is it true that we can know the event only through the experience of the church; we must also recognize that the church represents, as I have said, the sole residuum of the event. Nothing was accomplished by the event of which the church is not the embodiment or the promise. Since the beginning Christian theology has been concerned with what has been called the "work of Christ"—that is, with the purpose and issue of the event. What was God doing through Christ? We shall return to this question in the next chapter. Just now it is enough to say that if we may assume that God intended to accomplish what he did in fact accomplish, there can be no doubt as to what that was: he sought to bring into existence a new kind of human community—that kind of human community which the early church in the first instance and subsequently the church in all the centuries has, however inadequately, represented. If this was not his purpose, then must we not say either that the event of Christ had no purpose (at least so far as history is

48

concerned) or else that the purpose was not realized? For can we point to any other result of it? And if we say that God's purpose in Christ was an eschatological purpose (as in large part it undoubtedly was), a purpose the fulfillment of which lies beyond history, then we must also say either that we can have no conception at all of what that purpose was or else that it was the full realization in a new cosmic order of that community which is found so partially in the church.

The basis for these statements is the simple fact that the church is all we have—that is, all we have as Christians. It is true that we have the New Testament; but the New Testament is the creation of the community and brings us only the experience and thought of the community. To be sure, the New Testament has the unique value of giving us a kind of immediate access to the event as it originally occurred; but the event occurred only within the life of the primitive church and can be found only there. The New Testament gives us access to the event only because it makes us, in a real sense, participants in the experience of those to whom it was first occurring. As we read the New Testament, we become witnesses of the original event, not by getting "back of" or "beyond" the primitive community, but by getting more deeply into its life. For there is no access to the event except as it is remembered and embodied in the community.

It is also true that we have inner personal experiences of God's judgment and grace; but insofar as these experiences are distinctively Christian they take place within the context of the church's life and are possible only because we have shared in it with others. One may know the divine in some sense in one's solitariness or merely as a human being; but one cannot know the God and Father of our Lord Jesus Christ except where Christ

49

is found—within the historical community which emerged with the historical event and remains its sole resultant within history.[6]

II

Reference has been made to a new kind of human community which distinguished the early church and which constituted the principle of its unity as well as of its identity. The church, it has been intimated, *was* the church because it represented and in a degree embodied this community; and despite all diversities and divisions, it was essentially one for the same reason. What can we say as to the character and quality of this new community?

Before we make any attempt to answer this question, however, we must clarify somewhat the meaning of the word "community." If in this discussion we use the term in the way the early Christians used it, we shall not understand it to refer to the church or any other human group simply as such. The term normally means "sharing" or "partnership" and, it has been clearly shown,[7] invariably has this meaning in the New Testament. It is the sharing by a number of individuals in the same thing or things—a participation in a common reality. This being true, the relation of the church to the new kind of human community we are now to consider—if by "church" we mean an actual, definite, identifiable ("visible") society—must be expressed in some such way as: "The church, in some degree, represents [or "embodies" or "is characterized by"] the community." We cannot say that the church (in the sense just defined) *is* the community. It is because we sometimes use the word

---

[6] I would not want to be understood as overlooking the fact that Christ has exerted a strong humane influence upon culture generally; but this influence has been exerted, directly or indirectly, through the church.

[7] Most notably by J. Y. Campbell, "Κοινωνία and Its Cognates in the New Testament," *Journal of Biblical Literature,* LI (1932), 352-80.

"church" to refer to the common life itself and the word "community" to mean an actual organization of persons that our speech on this subject almost necessarily becomes involved in ambiguities and contradictions. If, for example, we mean by "church" the many actual groups in various lands organized and conducting their affairs in various ways, then the church is certainly not *one* and has never been; but if, when we speak of the church, we are speaking of the particular kind of shared experience that at least to some degree is characteristic of these various groups—if by "church" we mean the distinctive common life—then the church is one, indivisible, and everywhere the same. Since it is this shared experience, this community, which really constitutes the church, the church is eschatologically (or, if one prefers, ideally) all but identifiable with the community, and we can make such statements as, "Let the church be the church"; that is, "Let the church fully realize and express the community which makes it the church." Language being what it is, we can hardly avoid using the word "church" in both senses, and the same thing can be said of "community"; but for the sake of clarity, especially in this particular part of our discussion, it will be well to have in mind the distinction between the "church" in the ordinary sense and "community" in the stricter, more qualitative sense we have been trying to define. Our question, then, is what we can know about the character and quality of this community as it existed in the New Testament church.[8]

[8] Emil Brunner, in his book *The Misunderstanding of the Church* (London: Lutterworth Press, 1952), reserves the term "ecclesia" to designate what I am calling the new kind of community and uses "church" for the institutional or "visible" society. This is only a difference in words and has no importance; but I should take serious issue with Brunner's apparent assumption that primitive Christianity was pure "ecclesia" and that "church" with its faults and divisions was a later development. I should say that the

We may answer that the early Christian community was a sharing in a common memory and a common Spirit. The church's
self-consciousness might be analyzed into a consciousness of the
Spirit and a remembering of the event. The church was the
church—that is, it had its character as church in distinction
from other groups or societies—because the Spirit had been
given and because the event had transpired. The community was
participation in the corporate possession of the one and the corporate memory of the other. Both of these shared realities can
be dealt with only summarily in this chapter; and it must be
borne in mind at every stage that memory and the consciousness
of the Spirit, like the event and community, can be distinguished only for purposes of discussion; they were never actually
separated and cannot be.

Let us consider first the common memory. Because it is perhaps the simpler of the two elements and also because (I con-
fess) I have laid a good deal of stress on it in other writings,[9]
we shall devote less extended attention to it here. But this un-
equal treatment must not be allowed to obscure the full equality
of its importance. It is true that Christ was present in the early
church as the Spirit; that is, he was known as the living personal
center of the church's life. But he was also remembered as man
and Master. The two facts—he was known still and he was remembered—constitute together the miracle of the Resurrection;

distinction, and the discrepancy, between the community (as I have defined
the term) and the outward church (which I see no reason not to call
"ecclesia") are relevant in the early period as in any subsequent period.
The church as church has always been divided, at least in some degree;
the church as community has always been one (that is, of course, insofar
as it has existed as community).

[9] *The Man Christ Jesus* (New York: Harper & Bros., 1941); *Christ the Lord*
(New York: Harper & Bros., 1945), pp. 1-56; and *Criticism and Faith* (New
York and Nashville: Abingdon Press, 1952), pp. 33-44.

and neither is more important than the other. Without the one, early Christianity would have been a Jewish sect; without the other, it would have become a Gnostic cult. Whatever may be true of Christianity as it might have been, the memory of Jesus was an absolutely essential constitutive element in Christianity as it actually came to be.

Here lies the importance of the item in the creed to which reference has already been made,[10] "crucified under Pontius Pilate." How, it might be asked, does the name of a subordinate government official, belonging to a period already remote when the creed was written, get into the basic statement of the church's faith? Looked at in a certain way, the historical datum seems almost like an intrusion. But actually, of course, its inclusion is neither accidental nor irrelevant. It stands for the church's affirmation that Jesus Christ was no merely legendary person and that the events that happened to him and in connection with him were not the mere creations of fancy or faith. He was *remembered*. Perhaps it is not an accident that the historical dating, which confirms and symbolizes this fact in the creed, is introduced at the point of the Crucifixion. Not only was this (with the Resurrection) the crucial center of the event's significance;[11] it was also the focus of the community's memory of

[10] See pp. 47-48.

[11] Rudolf Bultmann, in *Kerugma und Mythos,* ed. H. W. Bartsch (Hamburg: Herbert Reich, 1951) , p. 44, sees the Resurrection as "the expression of the significance of the cross." It seems to me that Bultmann's failure to give adequate recognition to the community accounts for his failure to attribute a more objective reality to the Resurrection. Still, on somewhat different grounds than his I should agree that "cross and resurrection as 'cosmic' happenings are a unity." I would want to include in this unity other items also, indeed the whole remembered personality, career, and teaching of Jesus, as well as the coming of the Spirit and the rise of the church.

it. One is never so poignantly aware that another has lived, and of the whole concrete meaning of that person's life, as in the moment of his death; and the manner of Jesus' death would have made this especially true in his case. Luke and, to a degree, Matthew are interested in the date of Jesus' birth, and Luke provides a very elaborate dating of the beginning of his public ministry. But neither of these occurrences was remembered in the early church as the Crucifixion was—or rather, to say it better, Jesus himself was remembered in connection with his death as in connection with no other incident or phase of his career. This is the better way to say it for the reason that the memory we are considering was a memory of Jesus himself, not of any fact about him or of any word he spoke. The memory of the death came very near to being the memory of the man. One could not remember Jesus without thinking of his cross, or remember the cross without thinking of him. The very act of the church in which its remembrance of Jesus was supremely expressed and continuously renewed was an act in which his body was broken and his blood poured out, a proclamation "of the Lord's death until he come." The Supper was "in remembrance of his death and passion," but only because it was, more profoundly, in remembrance of *him*.

This memory of Jesus himself was a central element of the life of primitive Christianity and still belongs to the very being of the church. It has been conveyed from generation to generation as what Papias called, centuries ago, a "living voice." [12] This memory has been crucially supported and guarded by the Gospels and indeed the whole New Testament canon; but it would be a mistake to suppose that it has had through the centuries no independent existence, that what we are calling the

[12] Eusebius *Church History* III. 39. 4.

remembrance of Jesus is only an impression derived constantly afresh from the reading of the New Testament. One could just as plausibly argue that it is the remembrance of Jesus, belonging continuously to the life of the church, which in considerable part accounts for the impression which the New Testament documents make on us. As a matter of fact, the memory coming down through the generations in the living body of the church (supremely expressed in the recurrent sacrament of the Lord's Supper at the very center of both its worship and its common life) and the documentary records of the memories of the first generation—these belong inseparably together, confirming and enriching each other. Without the records, the church's memory would be far less firm and clear; but without the living memory, the records would be much less richly and concretely significant.

III

But the early church not only shared in a common memory; it also participated in a common Spirit. And on the reality, the meaning, and the importance of this Spirit I would want the major emphasis in the entire discussion of this book to fall. Not that the common Spirit was any more certainly indispensable to the existence of the church than the common memory; but its essential, constitutive character may perhaps be more easily ignored. It has already been intimated that differentiations in importance cannot be made between memory and Spirit. We have also been warned that the two belong inseparably together. If the event had not been remembered, the Spirit could not have come; but, without the Spirit, the event could not have been remembered just as it was remembered, for the reason that it could not have happened just as it did happen. For the event was, in its final issue, the coming of the Spirit. Only those who had received the Spirit could really remember the event, for it was only to them that the event had really occurred. But though the early church's remembrance of Jesus and its experience of the Spirit were actually inseparable, they can be distinguished in discussion; and so we come to the question: What was the "Spirit"?

At the beginning we must recognize that the Spirit, like the event, was something given; that is, the early church found itself possessing it. It was a concrete reality—something "poured out," "sent," "received"—not an idea in the mind or a conclusion arrived at by reflection. It was not an explanation of something or an inference from something; it was itself a fact which needed to be explained and from which inferences could be drawn.

I spoke just above of the "experience of the Spirit"; and it is of great importance to realize that when we speak of the Spirit in the early church, we are saying something, first of all, about its *experience*. Bultmann writes, about Paul:

"To be in the Spirit" no more denotes a state of ecstasy than "to be in Christ" is a formula of mysticism. Though Paul is familiar with ecstatic experience as a rare exception . . . ,[13] the Spirit, nevertheless, does not mean to him the capacity for mystical experiences. Rather, everything indicates that by the term "Spirit" he means the eschatological existence into which the believer is placed by having appropriated the salvation deed that occurred in Christ. To have received the Spirit means to be standing in grace.[14]

I am sure that Bultmann is right in denying that Paul's phrase "being in Christ" is a "formula of mysticism"; it is a reference to the new order of being, which is essentially eschatological but into which the believer is incorporated in principle even now.

[13] See on this point my *Chapters in a Life of Paul*, pp. 112-13.
[14] *Theology of the New Testament*, tr. K. Grobel (New York: Chas. Scribner's Sons, 1951), p. 335.

It is probably true that "to be in the Spirit" refers primarily to the same new status: one belongs, not to this age, but to the coming age of the Spirit.[15] We may also agree that the phrase does not denote a "state of ecstasy" if "ecstasy" is taken to mean a paroxysm or trance, such excitement or absorption as that the senses do not function and one loses all self-control. Although it is clear that Paul was at least occasionally subject to such experiences and that he attributed them to the Spirit—he could have done nothing else and been a child of his age—he certainly did not set great store by them and did not take them as representing any large part of the Spirit's activity. On the other hand, we must avoid the opposite extreme—namely, such objectifying of the Spirit as that it ceases to be the object of experience at all. The refrain of one of the most haunting of the Negro spirituals runs, "Every time I feel the Spirit moving in my heart. . . ." Is this "feeling" to be called "ecstasy"? That depends on our definition of terms. I should say that it is; surely there is rapture in it. But we do not need to argue about words. What I am concerned to say is that in the primitive church one *felt* the Spirit, and that the "feeling" was (for the person himself) unquestionable and unmistakable. The "Spirit" was not the object of belief merely, but also of knowledge, knowledge of the sort we have of concrete things; and the object of this knowledge was the very reality of God himself. The Spirit thus made himself known as God's Spirit, the Holy Spirit. This was true not only for Paul but for the early Christians generally.

This empirical character of the Spirit appears constantly in the New Testament. The question "How do you know you have received the Spirit?" would have seemed an utterly gratuitous and quite unanswerable question. The knowledge of the Spirit,

[15] See *Chapters in a Life of Paul*, pp. 128-40.

like our knowledge of concrete things generally, was self-authenticating—the basis of inferences, not an inference itself. The author of Luke-Acts tells how when Peter was preaching in Cornelius' house, "the Holy Spirit fell on all who heard the word" (Acts 10:44), and Peter asked, "Can any one forbid water for baptizing these people who have received the Holy Spirit just as we have?" The question whether they had received the Spirit was not raised. Later in the same work (Acts 19:1-6) Paul asked some "disciples" in Ephesus, "Did you receive the Holy Spirit when you believed?" They replied, "No, we have never even heard that there is a Holy Spirit." Paul then baptized them, and "when Paul had laid his hands upon them, the Holy Spirit came on them; and they spoke with tongues and prophesied"—again, a self-validating experience. Paul turns to his Galatian converts with "one question": "Did you receive the Spirit by works of the law, or by hearing with faith?" (Gal. 3:2). He can appeal to the reception of the Spirit as an indubitable fact of experience. And as he approaches the climax of his Letter to the Romans, he finds the source of the believer's confidence that he is a child of God, not in any argument about either God or man, but in the empirical fact that he finds himself crying, "Abba, Father." This spontaneous—may we not say ecstatic?—cry Paul attributes to the Spirit. One is "beside oneself" when one utters it. It is not one's own cry at all; it is the Spirit's—"the Spirit himself bearing witness with our spirit that we are the children of God." (Rom. 8:15 ff.) These examples have been taken from Acts and Paul; others, almost if not quite as impressive, could be found in the Fourth Gospel and the First Epistle of John, in Ephesians and First Peter. And these are the documents that reflect most richly the life of the primitive church.

It was this Spirit, an actual present possession, which provided the basis, the only basis, of the church's faith and hope. The faith (in the sense in which we are using the term in this discussion) [16] was the sure belief that in the event of Christ God had purposed to redeem us; and the hope was the confident expectation that he would "work his purpose out to its appointed end." But the event had already occurred, and the end had not yet come; the one was in the past and the other in the future. How, then, could faith be so sure and hope so confident? The answer was the actual presence of the Spirit. The Spirit had been given, and was the guarantee of the past and the promise of the future. It was more than that: the Spirit was the past actually continuing and the future already beginning. The Spirit was the living present which united past with future by participating in both—the witness to our redemption as sons and the earnest of our inheritance. Without the Spirit as a present empirical possession, the early church's faith and hope would have been impossible, at best pale abstractions without substance or ground. For the Christian faith is not mere faith; it rests on what we surely know. And Christian hope is not mere hope; it has already been partly realized. To speak of this partial knowledge, this partial realization, is to speak of the Spirit.

Paul makes this connection between the Spirit and our hope quite explicit in the familiar paragraph with which the fifth chapter of Romans begins. Having said that we rejoice "in our hope of sharing the glory of God," he goes on to promise that our hope will not disappoint us, "because God's love has been poured into our hearts through the Holy Spirit which has been given to us." Here the character of the Spirit as both experiential and evidential is fully implied. But a new note of great importance is also sounded: this is the virtual identification of the Spirit

[16] See footnote 1, above.

with "God's love." We will not claim that the phrase "love of God" has precisely the same meaning as the term "Spirit of God" any more than we would say that the words "Spirit of Christ" have the same meaning as the words "Holy Spirit"; but the same empirical reality is being referred to in each case. When God's Spirit is given, his love is being poured out. The word "poured" is significant in this connection. It suggests the richly concrete character of the love. The "love of God" is not merely a loving attitude of God toward us, of which we could at best become persuaded or convinced; it is God himself giving *himself* to us, to be actually received and enjoyed, to be known even more intimately and surely than one can know the love of a friend. God's love is not merely the disposition of *his* heart toward us; it is something "poured into *our* hearts." In a word, God's love is God's Spirit, and God's Spirit is his love.

I have spoken of the Spirit as the ground of faith and hope. Paul is not saying anything different when in the thirteenth chapter of First Corinthians he seems to give this basic position to love—"so faith, hope, love abide, these three; but the greatest of these is love." The chapter, it must be remembered, belongs to a discussion of the Spirit and its gifts: *agape,* Paul is saying, is more than a gift of the Spirit; it is the Spirit itself. The author of First John makes this identity explicit when he writes, "God is love" (I John 4:8); and the crucial evidential value of the Spirit is ascribed also to love when he writes: "We know that we have passed out of death into life, because we love the brethren" (I John 3:14).

For this love, which was the bond of union in the early church, was not ordinary kindness, good will, or affection, such as its members might feel and express in other relations also. It was a new thing. Perhaps we should understand the adverb in the

60

well-known remark reported by Tertullian, "See how these Christians love one another," [17] to mean more than "how much." Certainly it could have: a new kind of love had appeared in the world. This, of course, is the meaning of "the new commandment" in the Fourth Gospel and the First Johannine Epistle: "that you love one another" (John 13:34). The emphasis is not upon the fact of love or the identity of its objects, but upon its quality. The "commandment" is "new" because the love it commands is new.

The quality of this love, as of all concrete things, cannot be defined; it must be felt, and it can be expressed only in the forms of life and art. The Johannine writer indicates its quality only when Jesus says: ". . . even as I have loved you, that you also love one another." For this love was the love of Christ; it was the love that had drawn his disciples to Jesus, amazing them, sometimes frightening them, but holding them till it eventually conquered their pride and their loneliness, making them members of a new kind of brotherhood, sharers in a new Spirit. This new Spirit, which emerged with the event of Christ and was embodied in the community of Christ, could thus be called the Spirit of Christ. The living reality of this Spirit was the real ground of the resurrection faith. To know the Spirit was to know Christ, and in the most vital parts of the New Testament the terms can be used almost interchangeably. The resurrection of Jesus as an incident in time and space was an inference from, and became a symbol of, this identity. Christ, without ceasing to be the man and Master whose death was remembered, is now known as the Spirit; the event, without losing its character as historical event, is perpetuated in the community. This is the real and ineluctable miracle in Christianity. All other "miracles" are signs and

[17] *Apol.* 39.7: *"Vide, inquiunt, ut invicem se diligant."*

symbols of this one inexplicable but empirically given fact. The Spirit of the new community was no humanly generated comradeship; it was the very love of God poured out in Christ and uniting those who received it with one another because it united them also with him.

The whole purpose of God in Christ was the pouring out of this love, the giving of this Spirit. All the rich and varied phrases with which the early Christian evangelists sought to express the meaning of what God had done in Christ are ways of referring to this same thing: He has reconciled us to himself; he has overcome all hostility; he has adopted us as sons; "he has delivered us from the dominion of darkness and transferred us to the kingdom of his beloved Son" (Col. 1:13). In a word, the creation of the new community in Christ was the whole purpose of God. More, to be sure, was to happen; indeed, only the beginning had been seen. God's ultimate purpose was "bringing many sons to glory" (Heb. 2:10) —even more than that, the uniting of "all things in [Christ], things in heaven and things on earth" (Eph. 1:10). But the "good news" was not the mere announcement of a future fulfillment; something new had already happened. And it is what had happened that provided both basis and content for the early Christian hope. A new Spirit had come; a new love had been given; a new communal life had been brought into existence, a life incalculably rich not only because of what it promised but also because of what it was. For the Spirit was the Spirit of God; the love was God's own love poured out; the new life was his new creation. To share in this Spirit, this love, this life, was to belong to the church; the measure of one's sharing was the real measure of one's belonging. And in the unity of this Spirit, this love, and this life lay, and lies still, the church's essential and ultimately indefeasible unity.

CHAPTER THREE

THE   COMMON   FAITH

WHEN WE TURN FROM CONSIDERATION OF the memory of Christ and the experience of the Spirit to ask how the early church understood and interpreted what it remembered and experienced, it may well appear that we turn away from the principal, indeed the only deeply, unifying factor in primitive Christianity to consider the chief source of its conflicts and divisions. No one can deny the divisive role theological belief has often played in the history of the church, for the deepest divisions have been over issues of faith. Nor can it be doubted that there were wide and significant differences of belief in the early church and that these differences, in their own measure, constituted a constant challenge to whatever unity it had. But that is not the whole story; one would have to recognize also that theological belief constituted an important element in that unity. It is of the very nature of human life that wherever there is experience, there is also the effort to understand it; indeed, so close is the relationship that some reflection is integrally and essentially involved in experience itself. Our experience is the experience of thinking men, and can never itself be entirely dissociated from our thoughts about it. If the experience is a shared, a communal, experience, our thoughts about it will also be in some measure common thoughts; and this common element in our thinking will reinforce and enrich the communal character of the experience itself, confirming it as a bond of union.

We may be sure, then, that there could not have been the unifying life which we were considering in the preceding chapter unless there had also been a certain basic common faith; [1] and we should do less than justice to the unity in early Christianity if we did not attempt to identify it. The undertaking is precarious because of the large subjective factor that is always involved when one tries to differentiate between the essential and the nonessential, or the more and less important, elements in an actual complex whole. But since we are looking for the *common* and *distinctive* (as well as the basic) faith, objective criteria are not altogether lacking; and in any case the task cannot be avoided.

This basic common and distinctive faith was concerned primarily with Christ. The early church's questions about itself were questions about Christ. Its characteristic doctrine was a doctrine of Christ. Its theology was a Christology. This would inevitably have been true: it was Christ who had made all the difference; it was Christ who chiefly differentiated the Christian from both Jew and pagan. It was, then, the church's beliefs about Christ that constituted the essential and distinctive Christian faith. We do not need to say again that it is just these beliefs that have most frequently and deeply divided the church; what *may* require some clarification and emphasis is that there was in the beginning, and is still, a solid core of common christological belief—belief that not only does not divide us, but belongs to the very substance of our unity. We shall be seeking in this chapter to identify this "common core" especially in primitive Chris-

---

[1] Again, it must be recalled that we are using the term "faith" in only one of its senses. See footnote 1 in the preceding chapter.

tianity; but to find it there is to know where to find it in the later church as well.

I

One cannot gain even a little acquaintance with the early church—which means, one cannot do even a little reading in the New Testament—without recognizing not only the importance of what the word "Christ" stands for in its life, but also the richness and manifoldness of this same reality. In the brief discussion of this life in the preceding chapter I found myself necessarily alluding to Christ many times; and the complexity of the meaning of the term must also have appeared. He was referred to as a person remembered, but still known; and the miracle of the Resurrection was found in the inexplicable fact of this identity, undeniable because implicit in—indeed, primarily constitutive of—the very existence of the church. But sometimes the term was used in a way to suggest a reality more inclusive than a person, even this person. Often it was used to designate what we have been calling the event—that is, the whole complex of what happened in connection with Jesus (including the cultural setting and background, Jesus himself, his teachings, his relations with his disciples and others, his death, his resurrection, the coming of the Spirit, the creation of the church). But just as often the term was used to refer to the new community in the Spirit which the event made possible and in which it both culminated and is in a real sense continued. As a matter of fact, none of these three meanings—person, event, community—ever stands alone in Christian usage; all are present in some degree of relevance whenever the word "Christ" (or any equivalent term like "Jesus Christ" or "the Lord") appears. The word has this rich and varied meaning, not because one wants it to have it, or believes that it ought to have it, but simply because one cannot talk about the Christian life without using the term "Christ" in this manifold way. It would be easy to demonstrate this from any work of Christian devotion, ancient, medieval, or modern, and, most easily, from the New Testament itself.

It follows from this that the christological question does not need to be construed as a question about the person; it can just as appropriately be thought of as a question about the event or the community. And it is when we ask the question in one of the latter forms that the large and significant agreement in belief, not only among early Christians but among all Christians, is most likely to emerge. Let us suppose, for example, that we were accustomed to ask the question primarily about the event; that when we asked, "What think ye of Christ?" we meant, not "Who is he?" or "Whose son is he?" (Matt. 22:42), but "What has occurred? How are we to understand this thing that has happened among us?" If this were the question, would not the answer have been something like this: "In Christ, God has visited and redeemed us. The same God who made a covenant with Abraham has made a new covenant, calling into being a new people. He who made known his ways to Moses, his acts to the children of Israel, has acted now in the fullness of time to deliver mankind from all its enemies, from the guilt and power of sin and the fear and doom of death. This deliverance, although it can be fully consummated only in the age to come, God has brought about in our history and has made available in the new community of the Spirit to all who will receive it in penitence and faith." Would not this have been the unanimous early-Christian answer if the question had been asked in this form, and would it not have been the answer in every part of the church in all the ages since?

Or suppose the christological question had been primarily a

question about the community: "What is the reality in which these persons who knew Jesus and now remember him participate, and which constitutes the essential principle of the community's existence?" Would not the answer have been rather similar? Something like: "That reality is God's own presence and love—that is, his Spirit. Through the remembered event God has acted to bring into being this community, into which these persons have been called; in this community the One they remember is known as a living Presence, and in it are found the forgiveness, the healing, the security, the hope, they need. All of this is found there because God himself is present and active there and has chosen to bestow it there. It is the community of his Spirit." And would not this answer have been as unanimously given, through all the centuries, as the other?

In the actual course of christological reflection, however, the question (except possibly at the very first) has not been asked in either of these forms, and consequently the wide and deep agreement among all Christians about the meaning of Christ has been to some extent obscured. The characteristic christological question has been a question about the person: "Who was this person? What shall we call him? How shall we define his nature and his work? Whose son was he?" This preoccupation with the person can be partly explained by the fact that Christianity moved very early into a Greek environment. For the Hebrew it was natural to think of God as revealing himself chiefly in events occurring within a communal history; God had always made himself known primarily in mighty acts. The Greek, however, characteristically thought of revelation in less dynamic terms—as theophany, the appearance of the divine in human form. The Greek was also more interested than the Jew in speculative metaphysical questions, in questions about the nature of things, in distinctions between form and substance, and the like. But although such facts as these may help explain some of the directions that reflection upon the person of Christ took in the ancient church, they do not account for the initial emphasis upon the person. This emphasis was inevitable from the start. The event had centered in the person and career of Jesus, and the church's memory of it was largely a memory of him. The event had happened in and around him, and the community had come to pass among those who had known him. He was the divine personal center of the church's life (empirically identical with the Spirit). Moreover, the moment in which event and community met—the one culminating, the other emerging— was conceived of as the resurrection of this same person from the dead. All of this being true, it was inevitable, I repeat, that the christological question should have become almost at once a question about him and that the earliest statement of faith, the first "creed," should have been a statement about him.

The New Testament leaves us in no doubt both as to what that "creed" was and as to the unanimity with which it was accepted and used among the churches. It was: "Jesus is Lord and Christ." The constant collocation of these three terms in various parts of the New Testament—sometimes in the form of a quasi-creedal statement (as in Acts 2:36; Phil. 2:11), more often in such a phrase as "Jesus Christ our Lord" or "the Lord Jesus Christ"— bears witness to its prevalence. Thus, the common faith of early Christianity involved a considerable measure of agreement not only as to the significance of the event and the meaning of the community, but also as to the nature and role of the person: Jesus was Lord and Christ. It is important to note, however, that this agreement about the person was possible only because that category (that is, the person) was subordinate to the other two in the sense that the terms in which he was first defined were terms provided by the event and the community respectively

68

and constituted hardly more than a reassertion of the empirical values that the event and the community had proved to have. Only because this was true, we may believe, were the terms so unanimously acceptable. To call Jesus "Christ" and "Lord" was to say something about him, but only because it was to say something also about the event and the community. May I try to show that this is true?

II

First, then, to say that Jesus was "Christ" was to say something about the event. Now there can be no doubt as to the importance of Jesus in (or to) the event. The event happened around him; he dominated it completely. It was what it was in its concrete character in large part because he was what he was; and the memory of it was, as we have seen, largely the memory of him. All that was said in the preceding chapter about the church as a fellowship in memory needs to be carried in mind here. It is the massive fact that the event was completely dominated by the human figure of Jesus, which has always stood firmly in the way of every attempt either to mythicize the figure or to reduce its stature. An event of a highly distinctive kind and of incalculable creative power occurred in first-century Palestine; it was remembered as centering in and taking its character largely from a certain Jewish teacher and prophet. Contemporary, or almost contemporary, records confirm the memory both of the event as a whole and of the central and decisive position of Jesus within it. The fact that both the event and the community have, from the very beginning, been called by his name bears witness to this same centrality. No theory of Christian origins could be convincing either to the historian or to the believer which denied or even discounted the importance of the man Jesus in the event. No Christology which depreciated the person

69

of Jesus would stand now, or would ever have stood, a ghost of a chance of prevailing in the church.

But although it was undoubtedly the actual personal life and character of Jesus that in large part determined the actual concrete character of the event in the more objective sense, the relationship between person and event is, in a way, reversed when we consider the *faith* of the church. It was the meaning the event had proved to have in the experience of the primitive community that largely determined the earliest theological significance of Jesus. The situation in the early church was not that the event was regarded as the eschatological event because Jesus was believed to be the Christ, but rather that Jesus was called Christ because he had been the decisive center of what was empirically realized to be the eschatological event. The very first Christian theological question (essentially christological) was, "What has God done?" And the answer was (to repeat what has been said already in other words) : "He has reconciled the world to himself. He has put sin under sentence of doom. He has got us the victory. He has destroyed him who had the power of death. He has delivered us from the dominion of darkness. He has brought life and immortality to light. He has given us the kingdom." Now these are all descriptions of the eschatological fulfillment, for which other men had only wished, or at best only vaguely hoped. But for the early Christians, God had already acted to bring all this to pass. The consummation, to be sure, was still to come; but the thing had in principle been accomplished. He had already given his Spirit, the "guarantee of [their] inheritance," and they had already entered upon the experience of sonship. Their hope was not mere hope, but hope that had already begun to pass into realization. The final decisive event of human history had occurred. This was the empirical fact and was the real ground of the belief that Jesus was the

Christ. How could he not be when the event that he so completely dominated had proved to be the eschatological event? The statement of faith that Jesus was the Christ was really, in its basic intention, an affirmation that the event the church remembered was the supremely significant event of human history, God's final act of redemption.

But much the same kind of thing can be said also about the lordship of Jesus, as this was first affirmed. To say that Jesus was "Lord" was to say something about him, to be sure, but only because it was to say something about the community. It was a statement of belief only the shortest step removed from the actual experience of the church—hardly more than a description of that experience. No wonder it could be a common and universal faith. The earliest Christians found themselves belonging to a new community in which their memory of Jesus as human Master and Lord [2] was now reinforced and enriched by their knowledge of him as living and present in the church—still their Master and Lord, but in a new sense. Yet the sense was not altogether new. The hushed cry of one disciple to another when at the end of a long night of fruitless labor at their nets they see the risen Jesus on the shore, "It is the Lord!" (John 21:7), serves admirably to remind us of the continuity of the lordship of

[2] There is every reason to believe that the Greek term Κύριος was a translation of the Aramaic *Mar* (I Cor. 16:22), and that Jesus was called "Lord" before Christianity emerged into a Gentile environment, where Κύριος had its own religious connotations. See S. J. Case, "Κύριος as a Title for Christ," *Journal of Biblical Literature and Exegesis*, XXVI (1907), 151 ff.; and *The Evolution of Early Christianity* (Chicago: University of Chicago Press, 1914), pp. 116 ff.; B. W. Bacon, "Jesus as Lord" in *Jesus the Son of God* (New Haven: Yale University Press, 1911), especially p. 62; J. Weiss, *The History of Primitive Christianity* (New York: Wilson-Erickson, Inc., 1937), pp. 36-37; also V. Taylor, *The Names of Jesus* (London: Macmillan & Co., 1953). For the view that the "lordship" of Jesus is of Gentile origin, see W. Bousset, *Kyrios Christos* (Göttingen: Vandenhoeck & Rupprecht, 1913), pp. 77-104; R. Bultmann (*Theology of the New Testament*, pp. 52 ff.) takes the same position.

Jesus, as well as to suggest, at least, its fresh meaning after the Resurrection. They recognize him as their Lord—so they have called him all along—but now he is "the Lord" in a sense both more transcendent and more intimate. He is the ruler of the church just as he had been the leader of his little band of followers; he is the head (or, we would say, the heart) of the church just as he had been the center of interest and unity among them; he is the object of devotion, even worship, in the church just as he had been the object of his disciples' loyalty. But whether at one time or the other, to speak of Jesus as Lord was to speak of a relationship in which he stood to the community, and was to say therefore as much about the community as about him. He was "Jesus Christ *our* Lord." He could be known as Lord only by members of the community; or, to say precisely the same thing in different words, no one could "say 'Jesus is Lord' except by the Holy Spirit" (I Cor. 12:3).

We are dealing in these paragraphs with what I believe to be the most primitive faith. Once Christianity was established on Hellenistic soil, the term "Lord" tended to take its meaning primarily from its use to ascribe divine honors to emperors or to the gods who presided over the mystery cults, not to mention its use in the Greek Bible to render the unspeakable name of Yahweh. At the same time the word "Christ" tended to lose its meaning as the name of a function or office and to become a part of Jesus' own personal name. Thus, "Lord" came to carry something like the whole meaning formerly conveyed by the two names together. But in the beginning the titles were distinct and answered to the dual relationship (that is, with the event and the community) that we are now considering; and their primitive meaning was never completely lost. Jesus is still *the* Christ and *our* Lord.

As was pointed out in the preceding chapter, all early attempts to describe what is usually called the "work" of Christ are in the same way attempts to set forth the empirical realities of the new communal life. The "work" of Christ is the issue of the event. He is believed to have "overcome the world" and to have "condemned sin in the flesh" because in the new community the world is actually in principle overcome and the power of sin has been broken. He is believed to have "tasted death for every man," because the members of the community find themselves walking "in newness of life" and filled with the hope of "the life everlasting." He is "Savior," because the event has proved to be in fact the saving event and the community the saving community. All the earliest names of Jesus are functional names; they are ascriptions to him, as source or mediator, of the values that have been empirically received in consequence of the event and in the actual life of the community. They say only in various other ways that Jesus was Christ and Lord.

This Christ and Lord was, of course, believed in as divine. He was of "the nature of God"; he shared "the throne of God"; he was "at God's right hand"; he was "God's Son"; he was the divine "Logos." These terms cannot be pressed to yield definite and consistent conceptions of Christ's "nature"; if any such conceptions were formed in the earliest period, no one of them was generally shared. But they do indicate the common faith that the Lord of the church was, in effect, Emmanuel, "God with us." There is no convincing evidence that he was called "God" in the first century, and indisputable evidence that he was not generally called by that name; but it is clear that he was thought of as being related to God as no other man could be. But again this belief in the divinity of Jesus rested on the experience of the divine in the life of the community and on the recognition of the divine significance of the event. The position was not that the earliest Christians believed that the event and the community were divine because they also believed that Jesus was divine; but rather he was seen to be divine because of the way in which he was related to an event and a community whose divine significance was a matter of intimate and indubitable conviction. Must Jesus not have been divine to have been the center of so divine an event?

Not only was that the first way, it is also the true way, to ask the christological question, just as the true way to ask the question about the Resurrection is, "Must not Jesus have arisen from the dead, since he is the present living center of the church's life?" When the divine meaning of the event is made to depend upon views of Jesus' divinity and when the presence of Christ in the church is made to depend upon a belief in the Resurrection, we cut the solid ground out from under the whole Christian position; we invest the purely speculative with an importance it does not possess and rely on it to perform a function it cannot perform; and we open the door to discord and division. The common faith of the church—even though it is expressed in terms of belief about the person—rests always, and only, upon the common memory of the event and the common experience of the Spirit. On this ground the common faith of primitive Christianity was firmly based.

III

Thus far in this chapter two things have been attempted: first, to show that the primitive Christian faith could be a common faith because it was grounded in the very existence of the primitive church; and secondly, to indicate its basic structure. It was expressed, we have seen, in the formula: Jesus was Lord and Christ; that is, he was supremely significant in the community's own life ("Lord") and in human history ("Christ").

But this is only the basic structure of a faith which, even in New Testament times, underwent considerable development and was found in many diverse forms. This variety in early Christian belief was emphasized in the first chapter and will be alluded to again in the next, although in neither place does it suit the purpose of this book to describe it in any detail; it is the fact of this diversity that is of concern to us rather than the particular manifestations of it. But it is important that the fact be borne in mind even when we are discussing the "common faith." Only in basic structure was the faith common; as elaborated and articulated, it assumed a great variety of forms.

This was true because the church was not content to say simply that the event of Christ was, in the mysterious providence of God, the supremely significant event of history, since through it God had brought into being the new community of his love, in which sin and death are overcome and life and peace can be found—the community of the Spirit, of which the church is the anticipatory embodiment. It went on—inevitably, as things were—to ask *why* this particular event had had this particular effect; and this question, because it was a purely speculative question, unanswerable on the basis of the experience of the early church, was susceptible of almost as many answers as there were theologians to ask it. To raise this question is to assume that the secret of the significance of the event can be found within the event itself; whereas this secret lies in him who acted in and through it. One who raises this question of "why" must seek to answer it by breaking down the event and the new common life into their "parts" and then correlating the several elements of the one with the several elements of the other, as, for example, the death of Jesus with the forgiveness of sins; when really the event (like the new life itself) is one and indissoluble, and there is as little chance of our knowing the "why" of its effects as there is of our understanding why God does anything else he does in his creation in the precise way he does it. But speculation of this kind, for all its divisiveness, was inevitable; and agreement in the early church on what we have called the "basic structure" of faith did not prevent it.

On the other hand, the significance of this "basic structure" must not be minimized. Although it did not forestall or prevent the development of a wide range of diverse, and often conflicting, beliefs, nevertheless it did not fail to exercise a continuous and very powerful restraining influence. There are certain beliefs which the church, I think it is not too much to say, could never have accepted—beliefs which its very existence as the church would always have kept it from embracing, no matter how subtle the temptation or how potent the pressure. These beliefs would be formulated somewhat differently by different students of church history, and I would propose the following five statements as only approximately covering the field: (1) the church could not have denied the essentiality and the importance of its relations with Judaism and the Old Testament or its own being as the community of the new covenant; (2) it could not have doubted or denied the historical existence of Jesus; (3) it could not have minimized his significance; (4) it could not have denied his resurrection; and (5) it could not have surrendered its hope of his coming again. If true, these statements mean that the common faith of primitive Christianity (and of today) involves a wider area of agreement than we might at first suppose. May we briefly consider each of them?

First, then, we may say that the church could never have denied the essentiality and the importance of its relations with the Old Testament history and its own being as the community of the new covenant. This can be said because of the intrinsic nature of the event and because of its whole historical locus and nexus. It happened in the first instance among Jews, in the midst of a Jewish culture and in the course of Jewish history. The event of Christ is inconceivable in any other connection. Located anywhere else, it would have been a profoundly different—indeed, another— event. The difference would have consisted not simply in a different factual content, but, more important, in a different inner meaning. For the event of Christ was received and understood as a fulfillment of the age-old hopes and prayers of Israel, and this understanding entered integrally into the very existence of the event. It was *the* event because this kind of meaning was found in it. In Christ, God "remembered" his promises to Israel and, having renewed his covenant, was now fulfilling it. The church was the new Israel. Very early in its career Christianity moved into a Gentile environment, and new categories of interpretation, more or less alien to the Old Testament, were applied to it; but its primarily Jewish character persisted and was bound to persist. The Christian community was an organic development of the Hebrew-Jewish community.

This fact was constitutive and therefore undeniable. Marcionism, which sought to dissociate Christianity from Judaism, the new community from the old, with its doctrine of two Gods, the Creator-God of the Jews and the God and Father of Jesus entirely unknown to this world until Christ revealed him— Marcionism failed, not primarily because it proposed an unacceptable metaphysical theory, but because it denied an actual fact, the fact of Christianity's total connection with Judaism. The literature, lore, beliefs, and practices of the Jewish community had an important part in forming the Christian community; and the church's use of the Old Testament through all the centuries is only a sign of a connection with the Hebrew-Jewish community that is a profound, pervasive, and ineradicable characteristic of its whole life. The acknowledgment of this connection is a matter of common faith in the whole church, Catholic, Protestant, and primitive—a matter of common faith because, like every other element in that faith, it is no more, or less, than the recognition of what is actually and empirically true. It is firmly grounded in the very nature of the event and the community, an ineluctable implication of the very existence of the church.

In the second place, we may be sure that the church could never have doubted or denied the historical existence of Jesus. This impossibility also is implicit in the empirical reality of the event and the community, for it is of the very nature of the community to remember the event and the person around whom it occurred; and one simply cannot doubt the existence of what one remembers. One may acknowledge the possibility—even the likelihood or certainty—of mistakes in one's memory of the facts about a remembered person, but the existence of the person himself cannot be doubted. To doubt the existence of a person whom one has known well and now remembers would be to doubt one's own existence also. One's very identity is involved in one's trusting such memories. The question of the historicity of Jesus is a historical question, appropriate for the historian's consideration; but the Christian community, although it will have no doubts as to the outcome of any sound historical investigation into this question, will not be dependent on it for the answer. For its answer [3] is so deeply implicit in its life that it would never have occurred to it to raise the question at all. It would be impossible for the Christian community to entertain any lively doubt of Jesus' existence without in the same moment doubting its own existence. It is a historical community rooted in a his-

---

[3] On this point see pp. 52-55, 69-71, and my book *Criticism and Faith* (New York and Nashville: Abingdon Press, 1952), pp. 37-40.

torical event carried in its memory; to deny the memory would be to deny its own identity. It would cease to be this particular community—or, perhaps better, it would already have ceased to be—for the community involves by definition the sharing in a common memory. I have said that Marcionism was rejected, not because it proposed an unacceptable theory, but because it denied an empirical fact about the church. The same thing can be said about Docetism, which ascribed to the human life of Jesus only the appearance of reality. It too was unacceptable, not on philosophical, but on empirical, grounds. It was refuted, not by argument, but by the very existence of the church as a historical community.

It may be said, thirdly, that the church could never have minimized the significance of Jesus. This is true for the reason that, as we have seen, its understanding of the meaning of the event was from the beginning expressed in terms of a definition of the person of Jesus, and it would have been quite impossible for it to state that meaning in other than the highest terms it knew. He was at first (that is, after the Resurrection) Lord and Christ. As Christianity moved more fully into a Greek environment, these two titles were combined, as we have seen: "Christ" became a part of Jesus' own name, and its original meaning was taken over by "Lord," which was further enriched by its associations in the Greek Bible and in pagan religious usage, so that Paul could regard "Lord" as "the name which is above every name" (Phil. 2:9). Christological terms increased in number and in degree of exaltation: he was Savior; he was the Word or the Wisdom of God; he was the only begotten Son of God; he was God. The most important thing to be noted in connection with these and other names is not what the names themselves mean, but the fact that no name was deemed too exalted for Jesus. He must be given "the name which is above every name," whatever that name might in a given time and place seem to be. Whenever there was an issue as between possible names of Jesus or definitions of his person, it was the higher possibility that invariably carried the day. Thus, it was inevitable that the Christology of Athanasius should defeat Arianism.

Another example of the same principle is to be found, I think, in the adoption by the World Council of Churches of the requirement of belief in "Jesus Christ as God and Savior." Objection has often been raised to this formula; [4] as we have seen, it is not a characteristically biblical statement, and, moreover, it is theologically inadequate, since it ignores the humanity of Jesus. Furthermore, it appears to have been adopted originally without much deliberation, indeed almost by accident. But the later refusal to alter it in response to criticism illustrates the truth (which I believe the whole history of Christology will demonstrate) that where a greater or a lesser name is proposed for Christ, it is always the greater that is adopted. And this is true, I repeat, because the name of the person is really a symbol of the significance of the event; and the church finds it impossible to minimize that significance. The real question lying back of all speculations and controversy about the metaphysical nature of the person is the question: How important is the event? It is because the church, on the basis of its own experience, cannot set any limits whatever to this importance that it must inevitably accept for the person the highest name it can conceive for him. Thus, the rejection of Arianism rested finally on the same empirical grounds as the rejection of Docetism and Marcionism. All real heresies

---

[4] As, e.g., by C. T. Craig in *The One Church in the Light of the New Testament* (New York and Nashville: Abingdon Press, 1952) and, more fully, in his article "The Christological Foundation of the World Council of Churches," *Christendom*, XI (1946), 13-22.

are denials, just as all essential doctrines are affirmations, not of the church's opinions, but of its existence and its nature.

The two final statements in our proposed series can be dealt with even more quickly, because they have both been discussed somewhat already.[5] It was impossible that the church should ever have denied the resurrection of Christ, because its existence as the community of memory and the Spirit was the essential meaning of the Resurrection. To deny the Resurrection would have been to deny its own life as the community of the living Lord. And the same thing can be said of his coming again—the "coming again" being understood as a symbol of the final fulfillment of God's true and loving purpose for his creation, the "uniting of all things in Christ." This hope was implicit in the very existence of the community. Along with love and faith, it was *given,* an essential element in the actual life of the church. The Spirit, besides being the very breath of the community, the determining principle of its life, was also the inspirer and sustainer of an invincible expectation, "first-fruits" of the age to come, the "earnest of our inheritance." This ultimate, "eschatological" hope is inalienable and indefeasible, not because of rational argument or historical evidence (neither of these would be sufficient) , but because, as Paul says, "God's love has been poured into our hearts through the Holy Spirit which has been given to us" (Rom. 5:5) . This hope belongs to the very nature of the church, and the affirmation of it is therefore an integral part of our common faith.

It has not been the purpose of this chapter to define precisely the common faith of the early church or to indicate its limits, but rather to point to its existence and to suggest the proper method for discovering and identifying it. The common faith

[5] See pp. 59-62.

was an aspect of the unifying life. One could not share in the memory of the event and in the "communion of the Holy Spirit" without sharing also in certain beliefs; and the community of belief confirmed and strengthened the community of memory and Spirit, in which the beliefs found their source and ground. It is this threefold community which constituted, at the deepest level, the unity of the early church and still makes it possible, even in our divided churches, to speak of the holy Catholic church; and to speak of it not only as an object of hope and faith, but also as an already existing reality—a reality, indeed, in which we can have faith and for which we can hope only because we actually find it, deeper than our diversities and hostilities, in our midst and in our hearts.

THE BEGINNINGS
OF ORDER

ONE CANNOT HAVE FOLLOWED THIS book thus far with any degree of approval without being struck by the resemblances between the state of affairs in the early church and our own situation. We have seen that there was no single comprehensive organization of the churches; nor can a universal pattern of organization be traced among all the churches severally. There was no creedal statement (beyond the simple confession of the Lord Jesus Christ) universally acknowledged as binding and authoritative—indeed, there was great variety in both belief and worship. Not only was there no such thing as "organic union"; there was a great amount of regional, even local, independence, and conflicts and divisions among the churches were not infrequent. But such statements as these might belong to a description of contemporary Christendom. We have seen also that despite the variety and disunity in the early church, there were a deeply unifying common memory and common life and a surprisingly wide and significant common faith. But, again, have we not been reminded at almost every turn that we still share in this community of memory, of life, and of faith? Thus, that same contradiction between the essential unity of the church and the actual disunion of the churches, of which we are so painfully aware, existed then, too, and gave rise to the same kind of anxious concern.

But the correspondence goes even further: the ecumenical movement of modern times, in which we are seeking to overcome this contradiction through agreement upon common forms of polity, of worship, and of creed, has its parallel in the early Catholic movement, which had the same goal in view and was actuated by strikingly similar inner motivations and outward pressures. The inner motivations we have been considering in the last two chapters; and, because they constitute the really decisive factor, they will be of the greatest concern to us in this. The outward pressures were, of course, the propaganda of Gnostic teachers and the growing hostility of the Roman state (to both of which modern analogues are not far to seek). This ancient "ecumenical movement" belongs largely to the second century, most clearly to the latter half of that century; but its beginnings lie in the final decades of the first and therefore well within what may in the strictest sense be called the New Testament period. With these beginnings we shall be concerned in this chapter and the next.

I

At the outset we must lay some stress upon a fact which has been noted several times in the course of this discussion [1] but which thus far there has been no opportunity adequately to acknowledge—namely, the fact that early Christianity, even from the beginning, was not without many common features of organization and practice. We have devoted a chapter to the common life and another to the common faith of primitive Christianity; it would have been quite appropriate to include a similar dis-

[1] See pp. 21, 30.

cussion of common *forms*. And, indeed, that is what the earlier part of this chapter amounts to. As the unifying life implied inescapably a measure of common belief, so it implied a degree of conformity in polity and cult among the churches. And just as the common life was reinforced by the common faith, so, we may be sure, was it guarded and strengthened by this sharing in certain common features of organization and practice.

We have noted the prevalence of baptism as the rite of initiation into the Christian community and of the Supper of the Lord as the central act of its worship. Although there was undoubtedly great diversity in the New Testament period in the way these rites were administered and in the way their meaning was interpreted,[2] the fact of their general currency among the churches is an indication of a very significant degree of outward unity. It cannot be proved that either was observed absolutely everywhere in the primitive church; but the Synoptic Gospels and Acts manifestly reflect both practices, and the letters of Paul also take them for granted. Scholarly opinion is somewhat divided as to the attitude of the author of the Fourth Gospel toward these sacraments, but the most likely conclusion is that he fully accepts them; even if not, however, he bears witness, by his very efforts at correction or reinterpretation, to their general prevalence.

We do not know just how or when these rites began. The adoption of baptism as the symbol and means of initiation into the church must undoubtedly be understood in some connection with proselyte baptism in Judaism and with the use of the rite by John the Baptist, from whose followers some of the earliest of Jesus' disciples were drawn. The sacrament of the Lord's Supper, besides reflecting the universal, all but instinctive, recog-

---

[2] This was certainly true of the Supper. See H. Lietzmann, *Messe und Herrenmahl* (Bonn: Marcus & Weber, 1926) ; E. Lohmeyer, "Das Abendmahl in der Urgemeinde," *Journal of Biblical Literature,* LVI (1937) , 217-52.

nition of eating together as a symbol and means of fellowship, rests on the disciples' memories of meals with Jesus, pre-eminently the final meal, and perhaps also on the fact that some of the most decisive of their experiences of the risen Christ had occurred during the breaking of bread.[3] In the beginning, apparently, the common meal (significantly known as the Agape) can be distinguished from the special rite of the Eucharist, which took place in connection with it. For various reasons, not altogether clear, the Agape was given up, and only the Lord's Supper in the stricter sense remained.

But whatever the origin and early history of these rites, there can be no question as to their importance and as to the objective significance that was found in them. Baptism was an actual means of initiation, and the partaking of the Lord's Supper was an act of real participation in the body of Christ. The sharp distinction we often make between faith and Spirit on the one hand and the sacraments on the other undoubtedly reflects, in some degree, our modern individualism. For the early Christians the two elements, inner and outer, were bound inseparably and inextricably together in the corporate reality of the church.[4]

[3] See O. Cullmann, *Early Christian Worship* (London: S. C. M. Press, 1953), pp. 14 ff.

[4] We cannot go into any adequate discussion of the bearing in idea of these sacraments upon the reality and unity of the church. For an excellent brief statement, especially for Paul, see Stig Hanson, *The Unity of the Church in the New Testament* (Uppsala: Almquist & Wiksells, 1946), pp. 75-90. One may also consult with great profit J. A. T. Robinson, *The Body: A Study in Pauline Theology* (London: S. C. M. Press, 1952) and "The One Baptism as a Category of New Testament Soteriology," *Scottish Journal of Theology*, VI, 257-74; and W. Norman Pittenger, *The Christian Sacrifice* (New York: Oxford University Press, 1951). See also W. F. Flemington, *The New Testament Doctrine of Baptism* (London: Society for Promoting Christian Knowledge, 1948); O. Cullmann, *Baptism in the New Testament* (London: S. C. M. Press, 1950); G. W. H. Lampe, *The Seal of the Spirit* (New York: Longmans, Green & Co., 1951); George Johnston, *The Doctrine of the Church in the New Testament* (Cambridge, 1941); C. T. Craig, *The One Church in the*

The sacraments do not stand alone, of course, as outward marks of primitive Christianity. The observation of the first day of the week as the "Lord's Day" in a special sense; the widespread, if not universal,[5] use in public worship of hymns and chants voicing worship of Christ and of readings from the Jewish Scriptures; various similar, if not identical, prayers; the recalling of the words of the Lord and of the significant events of his career in preaching and teaching—these were among the more important features of the early Christian cult which had the effect of outwardly distinguishing a group of Christians, wherever they might be found, from their neighbors and of confirming their unity among themselves and with other Christian groups. Equally important as a mark of the Christians was their repudiation, or at least avoidance, of prevailing pagan rites. One must also recognize, as common features of the greatest significance, the respect for Jerusalem widely prevalent among the churches and the general acknowledgment of the authority of the apostles. These two characteristics of early Christianity will be discussed at some length later in this chapter.

Still, despite these resemblances and common loyalties, it is clear, as we have seen, not only that there was no inclusive and centrally administered organization—no one "visible" institutional church united under hierarchy or council—but also that

---

Light of the New Testament (New York and Nashville: Abingdon Press, 1951), pp. 67-94; A. J. B. Higgins, *The Lord's Supper in the New Testament* (London: S. C. M. Press, 1952); R. R. Williams, *Authority in the Apostolic Age* (London: S. C. M. Press, 1950), pp. 89-103; V. Taylor, *The Atonement in New Testament Teaching* (London: Epworth Press, 1940), pp. 236-42; C. C. Richardson, *The Sacrament of Reunion* (New York: Chas. Scribner's Sons, 1940), pp. 75-99; E. S. Sjöberg, "The Church and the Culture in the New Testament" in A. Nygren *et al.*, eds., *This Is the Church* (Philadelphia: Muhlenberg Press, 1952).

[5] See pp. 25-27.

discordant variety, and occasionally even division and schism, sometimes prevailed.

I have spoken of the "anxious concern" that divisions in the early church occasioned some of the more responsible and sensitive leaders; and perhaps as good a way as any of observing the beginnings of the Catholic movement is to note the evidences of this concern in the New Testament. I have already cited some of the relevant passages with a view to demonstrating the existence of tensions or divisions; [6] now, in this and the following chapter, I should like to examine them more thoroughly with a somewhat different purpose. Taking the New Testament documents as representative of the thought of the early church, what can we say as to the extent and kind of interest its leaders felt in its unity? Although other documents of the New Testament, as of the Apostolic Fathers, are concerned with this issue and will be referred to in the course of our discussion, we shall give largest attention to the letters of Paul, which, as written, are our earliest sources for the primitive church and, as collected, represent the first and perhaps the most decisive phase in the so-called Catholic movement.

II

We have already referred to the frequency with which Paul expresses his concern for the unity of the several congregations to which, from time to time, he is writing. One finds a surprising number of passages of this kind when one reads the letters with this particular point in mind. The Roman church Paul does not know very well; but he apparently knows it well enough to be sure that he can appropriately devote almost the whole of the final or "practical" section of his letter to an appeal for love

[6] See pp. 34-36.

among the brethren there. They are to recognize themselves as members of "one body"; and each is faithfully and humbly to contribute his particular "gift," not thinking of himself "more highly than he ought to think." The strong are to be patient with the weak, and those with certain scruples about food and such matters must be tolerant toward those who do not have them or have different ones. They are not to please themselves, but each is to "please his neighbor for his good, to edify him." As for First Corinthians, it is not necessary to remind ourselves again how completely it is dominated by this same concern.[7] Though this concern is less explicit in Second Corinthians, it is hardly less important there: in chapters 10–13 Paul is fighting for the unity of the Corinthian church, in loyalty to the gospel, as certainly as for his own standing in its regard; and chapters 1–9, whether earlier or later than 10–13, are a celebration both of its return to loyalty to him and of its recovery (he hopes) of the unity it had lost.

The same interest is manifest in the shorter letters. Galatians, although wider issues are at stake, is under one of its aspects a bitter protest against the activities and views of those who threatened to divide the Galatian church; and in 5:20 "dissension" and "party spirit" are specifically condemned. The recurring emphasis to the Philippians is the "one spirit" and "one mind" they are to have (1:27; 2:2). Here again is a warning against the schismatic Judaizers (3:2 ff.). Euodia and Syntyche are entreated to "agree in the Lord" (4:2). The concern that the whole church be "in full accord" and its members free from "selfishness or conceit" calls forth the great christological passage (2:5-11) celebrating the self-sacrifice of Christ and his present

[7] See p. 35.

exaltation as the Lord of all. Colossians is obviously partly occasioned by the threat to the unity of the body of Christ which Paul sees in certain Gnostic views then current in Colossae. Not only must the members of the church there hold "fast to the Head, from whom the whole body [is] nourished and knit together" (2:19), but they must also forbear and forgive one another and "above all ... put on love, which binds everything together in perfect harmony" (3:13-14; compare 2:2). The Thessalonian letters are perhaps less explicit on this point, but no less certainly concerned with it, as I Thess. 5:12-13 makes clear: "But we beseech you, brethren, to respect those who labor among you and are over you in the Lord and admonish you, and to esteem them very highly in love because of their work. Be at peace among yourselves."

This last passage will remind us that, for all his reliance on the Spirit, Paul clearly saw the part discipline must have in preserving the unity of the congregation. Those "who labor among you and are over you in the Lord" are to be respected. The disobedient, we learn from the same letters, are to be warned and, if they persist, are to be excluded (compare I Cor. 5:13). It is not clear just who the administrative officers of the Pauline churches were (that is, of course, under Paul himself) and how they were named. Were "those who are over you" placed there by Paul or by vote of the congregation, or did they come to exercise their administrative functions simply in virtue of endowment and consecration (that is, "by the Spirit")? In I Cor. 12:28 Paul seems to be indicating a certain hierarchy of functions: "God has appointed in the church first apostles, second prophets, third teachers, then workers of miracles, then healers, helpers, administrators, speakers in various kinds of tongues." Where in this list do "those who are over you" belong? One would suppose they were the "administrators," except for the strangeness of finding subordinate gifts apparently conferring superior authority.

In the same letter, besides implying the existence of a class of adminstrators by the directions he gives the congregation (which some person or persons must enforce), Paul explicitly refers to Stephanas and others as men to whom the church is to "be subject" and "give recognition" (I Cor. 16:15-18). It is noteworthy, perhaps, that in this passage the persons to whom this deference is due are identified as "laborers," as men who "have devoted themselves to the service of the saints." Also in I Thess. 5:12-13 the men whom the church is to "respect" are "those who labor among you"; they are to be esteemed "very highly in love because of their work." Is it not likely, then, that administrative authority in the local Pauline churches was at first not vested in any formally named or ordained class but belonged automatically to those who were actually doing the greater part of the work of the church? Weizsäcker, in speaking of Paul's directions about Stephanas and others in I Cor. 16:15-16, writes:

According to this there were a number of people who were to be regarded as superintendents in the church. The claim was based on their having been the first to believe and on their maintaining the church by their ministry. The Apostle's exhortation shows accordingly that . . . it was not a question of an office that had been instituted, but of a relationship that had grown out of the facts, a relationship founded constantly on voluntary work and dependent on the good will of the community.[8]

This being true, the terms "bishops" and "deacons" in Phil.

[8] *Apostolic Age* (London: Willims & Norgate, 1899), II, 320. See also the note on "Ruler" in B. S. Easton, *The Pastoral Epistles* (New York: Chas. Scribner's Sons, 1947), pp. 221-28, and H. von Campenhausen, *Kirchliches Amt und geistliche Vollmacht in den ersten drei Jahrhunderten* (Tübingen: J. C. B. Mohr, 1953), pp. 72-75.

1:1 may refer, not to two distinct classes of formally ordained officers, but to the core of workers in the Philippian church who were rulers ("bishops") because they were also servants ("deacons"; compare I Cor. 16:15-16), and who did not cease to be servants because they were rulers as well. Or perhaps the two terms distinguished the older and more mature from the younger church workers. But however the several questions raised in this paragraph should be answered, it is clear that Paul recognized the need of an established ministry of some kind in his several churches if the disorder and disunion he deplored were to be avoided.

But Paul's concern for unity goes beyond the congregation; he manifestly thinks of himself as possessing a certain authority in all his churches and expects them to conform, at least in some degree, to a common type. He seeks to exercise his authority in ways that will not jeopardize or impair the freedom of his congregations; but he does not fail to exercise it. At the time First Corinthians is being written he has just sent or is about to send Timothy to Corinth (4:17) "to remind you [he tells them] of my ways in Christ, as I teach them everywhere in every church." After laying down certain rules about the dress and behavior of women in the services of the church (11:2-15), he warns, "If any one is disposed to be contentious, we recognize no other practice, nor do the churches of God." [9] A similar point is made and the same example is invoked in 14:33-34: "As in all the churches of the saints, the women should keep silence in the churches"; and Paul concludes with: "What! Did the word of God originate with you, or are you the only ones it has reached?" Earlier he has said—more tenderly, but perhaps

[9] On this phrase see p. 97. See also C. T. Craig, *The One Church in the Light of the New Testament*, p. 45.

more coercively on that account—"Though you have countless guides in Christ, you do not have many fathers. . . . I became your father in Christ Jesus through the gospel."

He evidently expects his various congregations to have a fellow feeling with one another. He tells the Thessalonian church of the great interest other churches have in it, even saying that the Thessalonians have become "an example to all the believers in Macedonia and in Achaia" (I Thess. 1:7). His churches greet one another through Paul (I Cor. 16:19; II Cor. 13:13; Phil. 4:22). He and his associates were constantly visiting among the churches, conveying information and greetings and undoubtedly creating a sense of peculiar community. Paul expects all his churches to be loyal to him—he is their only "father" (I Cor. 4:15)—and this common loyalty to him would involve mutual loyalties also. He encourages hospitality.[10] The offering for the poor at Jerusalem, about which we hear in Galatians, First and Second Corinthians, and Romans, and of which we must speak again in another connection, was a great co-operative undertaking among the Pauline churches. Paul appeals to the Corinthians to match the generosity of the Macedonians (II Cor. 8:1-7), just as he has apparently challenged the Macedonians with the example of the Corinthians (II Cor. 9:2). Common methods of taking the offering were followed in the several churches, or at least Paul hoped that they might be: "As I directed the churches of Galatia, so you also are to do," he writes the Corinthians (I Cor. 16:1). And when the contributions of the several churches are complete, their representatives are to assemble and accompany one another to Jerusalem to deliver the fund as a

[10] Rom. 12:13 and also, if genuine, Rom. 16:1 ff. On the extent and importance of hospitality in the early church generally see D. W. Riddle, "Early Christian Hospitality: A Factor in the Gospel Transmission," *Journal of Biblical Literature*, LVII (1938), 141-54.

corporate gift. In a word, it is clear that Paul was not simply the founder of separate congregations. He was also the organizer and administrator of a large body of congregations; and although we should have no right to suppose that he achieved, or even sought, absolute uniformity of polity and usage among them, he was concerned to promote harmonious relations among them in every possible way and almost certainly he expected a general conformity to a common pattern.

But this concern of Paul went further still. In our discussion [11] of the conference of Paul with the leaders at Jerusalem (referred to in Gal. 2:1-10 and Acts 15:1-29) it was pointed out that, from Paul's point of view, one of the most important issues at stake was that of the unity of the church—the whole church. As the matter was formally presented to the conference, the question at issue was simply whether the redemption in Christ could be acknowledged as available to uncircumcized Gentiles. Or, to state the question differently: Are Gentile Christians, or prospective Gentile Christians, free of obligation to the ceremonial requirements of Judaism? Paul, of course, was eager that the Jerusalem "pillars" should give an affirmative answer to *this* question; but this was not, I should say, the question of greatest personal concern to him. His own question was: Will believing Gentiles be accepted as belonging to the church in the same way as Jewish believers, sharing fully with them in one body? It was this doubt as to whether the principle of the *unity* of the church was to be recognized which drove him to Jerusalem "lest . . . [he] should be running or had run in vain" (Gal. 2:2). The incident at Antioch (Gal. 2:11-14), when one of the "pillars" withdrew from table fellowship with the Gentile believers at the instigation of another of the "pillars," would have told

[11] See pp. 38-41.

him that the conference had not given as firm and clear an answer to *his* question as he had hoped.

It was the urgency of this question that accounted for the energy with which Paul devoted himself to the offering for the poor of Jerusalem to which reference has been made. The conference with the "pillars" had made no formal requirement of the Gentile churches in Paul's area except that they "remember the poor." Paul undoubtedly found this a most congenial request— for what could be a more fitting token of unity than a really substantial offering, and what could promote it more effectually? For several years, we may believe, this offering was Paul's major preoccupation. When it was finally complete, it was dispatched to Jerusalem in the care of a large and representative delegation from the Pauline churches (compare I Cor. 16:3 and Acts 20:4); and although Paul was very eager to proceed toward Rome and Spain (Rom. 15:23-29; Acts 19:21) and although he had reason to fear actual danger to his person at Jerusalem (Rom. 15:31; Acts 21:10-14), nevertheless he decided that he must accompany this delegation. Clearly this offering was more than a simple philanthropic act; it had very important ecclesiastical, almost theological, implications. It was a symbol of the unity of the church.[12]

One must see in it also a sign of Paul's recognition of the debt of loyalty the Gentile churches owed to the Palestinian Jewish churches. He says as much in explaining the purpose of the offering in his Letter to the Romans: "If the Gentiles have come to share in their [the saints at Jerusalem] spiritual blessings, they ought also to be of service to them in material blessings"

---

[12] See my *Chapters in a Life of Paul*, pp. 52-58. See also J.-L. Leuba, *The New Testament Pattern*, Tr. H. Knight (London: Lutterworth Press, 1952; French edition, 1950), pp. 119-20. Also Bultmann, *Theology of the New Testament*, Tr. K. Grobel (New York: Chas. Scribner's Sons, 1951), p. 61.

(15:27). But there is no lack of other indications that Paul, for all his insistence upon the equality of all men, regardless of race, in Christ, still regarded the Jew as having a certain priority, if not advantage. As I have said, the Judaizers had no difficulty in "reading" the Gentiles out of the church, but Paul would have found it impossible to "read" the Jews out. The original Christians had been Jews, and Gentiles had become Christians by being permitted to share in what the Jews already possessed. The gospel was "the power of God for salvation . . ., to the Jew first . . ." (Rom. 1:16). Not only had this been the actual order; it was inevitable that it should have been. To the Jews "belong the sonship, the glory, the covenants, the giving of the law, the worship, and the promises; to them belong the patriarchs, and of their race, according to the flesh, is the Christ" (Rom. 9:4-5). Paul in controversy with Judaizers may in effect have denied this advantage to the Jew (as in Galatians), but he was unable to sustain such a position (see Rom. 3:1 and 11:1-32). The facts, as we also must recognize, were against it. Salvation was indeed "from the Jews" (John 4:22). The Jewish nation, to be sure, had apparently rejected the gospel; but a remnant had not done so, and this remnant was a token of the eventual redemption of the nation: "All Israel will be saved" (Rom. 11:26). It could not be otherwise in the light of God's promises to Israel. Meantime the temporary apostasy of Israel was being providentially used to make the gospel known to the Gentiles. But the root of the church was a Jewish root, and the "mother of us all" was Jerusalem—a Jerusalem "above" but still Jerusalem (Gal. 4:26). Paul's going up to the city for the conference was an acknowledgment not only of his desire for harmonious relations with the church of Judea, but also of his recognition that in the very nature of the case it enjoyed a certain pre-eminence among the churches.[13] The many evidences that Paul did not regard this pre-eminence of the Judean church as implying a legal authority over the Gentile churches must not be allowed to obscure the many indications that he recognized the pre-eminence itself and the spiritual leadership it conferred.

III

Another factor confirming and in a degree defining Paul's conception of the unity of the church was his firm faith in apostolic authority, concerning which, as it applied particularly to himself, something has already been said. In the list of church officers in I Cor. 12:28 the "apostles" are named first. Paul bases his right to direct his churches on the fact that he is an apostle; and even in approaching the unknown church at Rome, although he clearly wants to be irenic and to avoid every appearance of presumption, he does not hesitate to appeal to this same fact (1:1, 5-6). Now the term "apostle" was a common word meaning "one sent"—an ambassador or envoy—and there is no question that in the early church it was sometimes used to designate any authorized traveling evangelist (see, e.g., Didache 11:4-6 and, I should say, Acts 14:4, 14). It is commonly said that this was the earlier use of the term in the church and that

[13] J.-L. Leuba (*The New Testament Pattern*, pp. 122-23) argues (following Holl ["Der Kirchenbegriff des Paulus in seinem Verhältnis zu dem der Urgemeinde" in *Gesammelte Aufsätze zur Kirchengeschichte* (Tübingen: J. C. B. Mohr, 1928), pp. 44 ff., especially 58 ff.] and others) that the expression οἱ ἅγιοι ("the saints") meant, for Paul as well as generally, the churches of Judea (see Rom. 15:25, 26, 31; I Cor. 16:1; II Cor. 8:4; 9:1, 12 [cf. Acts 9:13, 32, 41; 26:10]). His case would be stronger if Jerusalem were not *mentioned* (rather than being unmistakably implied) in so many of these passages; in other words, it is not clear that οἱ ἅγιοι alone would have been understood as referring to the Judean believers. I Cor. 16:15 seems to indicate the contrary; but one cannot be sure. Leuba interprets "all the churches of the saints" in I Cor. 14:33 as a reference to the churches of Judea and also in the same way "the churches of God" in I Cor. 11:16 (*op. cit.,* pp. 123-24).

the reservation of it for a very restricted group (as for the Twelve) was a later development. Thus Bultmann can write that "Paul calls all missionaries apostles." [14] But the evidence that he did so is meager and unconvincing. None of the passages cited by Bultmann needs to be interpreted as referring to "apostles" in the broad sense.[15] On the other hand, how can we explain Paul's insisting so repeatedly and vehemently on the authenticity of his apostleship if any missionary was an "apostle"? How, indeed, could the issue of his apostleship ever have arisen if that had been the meaning of the term in the early church, or at any rate with Paul? At the least we must say that if Paul occasionally used the word to mean simply a missionary, he did not use it thus very often or most characteristically. An "apostle" was a missionary who was such because he had seen the Lord

[14] *The Theology of the New Testament*, p. 60. See also Foakes-Jackson and Lake, eds., *The Beginnings of Christianity* (New York: The Macmillan Co., 1933), V, 37-59; and article on ἀπόστολος in Kittel, *Theologisches Wörterbuch zum Neuen Testament*.

[15] These passages are I Cor. 9:5; Rom. 16:7; II Cor. 11:5, 13, and 12:11-12. As for I Cor. 9:5, there can be no assurance that the word "apostles" is not being used in the restricted sense. In Rom. 16:7 it is barely possible to argue that the intention is that Andronicus and Junias were men of note *in the regard of* the apostles; but the authenticity of the passage, however understood, is not above question (see *Interpreter's Bible*, IX, 365-68). II Cor. 11:5, 13 and 12:11-12 all refer to "apostles" in some depreciatory connection; Paul may be denying their right to be called apostles at all, or, in the heat of battle, he may be affirming that, though apostles, they are not worthy of their vocation or are perhaps asserting themselves in areas where they have no authority.

The clearest instances of a use of the term by Paul in the general or broad sense are II Cor. 8:23, where he speaks of certain "brethren" as "messengers [ἀπόστολοι] of the churches," and Phil. 2:25, where Epaphroditus is referred to as "your messenger [ἀπόστολος] and minister to my need." But in both these cases, the "apostles" are apostles *of churches,* not "of Christ." It can be plausibly argued that when Paul uses the term "apostle" without qualification of any kind, he means one of the very limited number whom the risen Christ has directly and specifically called into his service.

(I Cor. 9:1) and had been summoned to his work by Christ himself.

We do not know just who in Paul's view the apostles were, except that he and Peter were among them. Only one reference to "the twelve" is found in the letters (I Cor. 15:5), and in view of the importance of the Twelve in later tradition much dependence cannot be placed upon a single reference.[16] Anton Fridrichsen, relying on Gal. 2:7-8, where Paul speaks of the "gospel of uncircumcision" as intrusted to him in the same way as the "gospel of circumcision" was intrusted to Peter, suggested that Paul acknowledged only two effectual, or really important, apostleships—his own and Peter's.[17] But this view, in many ways attractive, cannot be easily harmonized with Paul's words in Gal. 1:17, 19, and elsewhere.[18]

In any case, however, we can be sure that for Paul "the apos-

[16] J. Weiss regards "then to the twelve" in this passage as an interpolation. See his commentary on First Corinthians, p. 330, and *The History of Primitive Christianity*, ed. F. C. Grant (New York: Wilson-Erickson, Inc., 1937), I, 24.

[17] "The Apostle and His Message," *Uppsala Universitets Årsskrift*, 1947.

[18] Still the suggestion deserves serious consideration that Paul conceived of himself as *the* apostle to the Gentiles and of Peter as *the* apostle to the Jews. The Epistle to the Romans is interpreted as an attempt to "assert, in a discreet way, the apostolic authority and teaching of Paul in the church at Rome. . . . The Epistle to the Romans is probably one link in an extensive correspondence of Paul's with the non-Pauline churches of the Mediterranean." Fridrichsen does not ask the question (at any rate in the article under consideration); but one is bound to wonder whether this can be the explanation of some of the textual phenomena of Romans, particularly the omission from some manuscripts of "Rome" in chapter 1 and of chapter 15. In that case, while the only surviving form of the letter was the form that went to Rome, there would have been a shorter, more general form which went to other non-Pauline churches. This letter would have been sent, in most cases probably, in lieu of a visit rather than in anticipation of one. After all, Paul does not in Rom. 1 actually announce or even promise a visit; he speaks only of his desire to come. The actual announcement is found only in chapter 15. This hypothesis would also explain what is otherwise the strange absence of any reference to Spain in chapter 1.

tles" were a small and closed group. They had been appointed by Christ himself, and they exercised, under him, the highest authority in the areas of the church in which they severally served. Within those areas they performed a unifying function; and insofar as they agreed with one another—and to a large extent, we may believe, they did—they contributed to the deepening of mutual confidence and loyalty among the churches and to the creation and growth of common forms of creed and cult.

CHAPTER FIVE

THE GROWING UNITY

IN THE PRECEDING CHAPTER WE WERE NOT-
ing the signs in the several letters of Paul of his concern about
the peace and unity of the church—the peace and unity not
only of each local church, but also of the churches in their relations with one another. It seems clear, however, that whatever
influence the letters may severally have had, their weight was
most fully felt only when some person or group collected them
and made them available to a wider audience in book form.
This collection has a bearing of great importance upon the
growing unity of the church, and we may appropriately resume
our discussion of the early Catholic movement with some consideration of it.

I

It is beyond dispute both that Paul's letters were collected
and that the collection had been made before the middle of the
second century, since Marcion is known to have possessed it then.
Zahn, Harnack, Goodspeed, apparently Johannes Weiss, and
many others would date it toward the end of the first century.[1]

[1] T. Zahn, *Die Geschichte des neutestamentlichen Kanons* (Erlangen:
A. Deichert, 1888) , I, 837; A. Harnack, *Die Briefsammlung des Apostels Paulus
und die anderen vorkonstantinischen Christlichen Briefsammlungen* (Leip-

The contents of this first formal collection are indicated almost as clearly as its early date: Romans, First and Second Corinthians, Galatians, Ephesians, Philippians, Colossians, First and Second Thessalonians, and Philemon—that is, all the letters attributed to Paul in the New Testament except the Pastoral epistles. The study of this collection raises many problems too complicated for consideration here; but fortunately we do not need to consider them. The fact of the collection (by whatever process or agency) does not need to be demonstrated; its exact date, since it could not have been later than the middle of the second century, can for our purposes be left open; only the occasion and motive of the collection concern us here.

The most important motive was unquestionably veneration for the apostle and the conviction that what he had written was permanently true and of great significance for the church. Paul's own contemporaries, even his enemies, had recognized that his letters were "weighty and strong" (II Cor. 10:10); but now, a generation after the apostle's death, they were not receiving (some disciple of Paul decided) the attention they deserved. Perhaps even a church like Corinth or Colossae, to which a letter of Paul had been actually sent, was showing that it did not appreciate the treasure it possessed; much less could be expected of other churches, many of which, indeed, would never have seen a letter of Paul. Moreover (this unknown "Paulinist" may have reflected), adequate appreciation of a single letter of Paul would in any event be impossible if one knew it alone; only if collected and presented together could the letters of Paul have their true effect. Only if one read a number of Paul's letters and interpreted each in the light of the others could one really

---

zig: J. C. Hinrichs, 1926), p. 7; E. J. Goodspeed, *New Solutions of New Testament Problems* (Chicago: University of Chicago Press, 1927), pp. 1 ff.; J. Weiss, *History of Primitive Christianity*, II, 682.

understand "the stewardship of God's grace that was given to [him], . . .the mystery . . . made known to [him] by revelation, . . . [his] insight into the mystery of Christ" (Eph. 3:2-4). The collection was undoubtedly a tribute to Paul and a testimony to the continuing truth and importance of what he had to say.

But there is another phase of the significance of the collection which is almost as important. The Pauline letter corpus reflects a situation of growing outward unity among the churches and must be recognized as being, under one of its aspects, an effort to promote it. What had been letters, some of them short and almost casual, to a number of scattered congregations has now become a massive and impressive message to the whole church. It is not unlikely that the corpus was laid out in a seven-part form,[2] just as we have the "seven churches" of Asia in Rev. 1-3; and if this is true, the intention was presumably to suggest the universality of the church addressed in the corpus as a whole. Certainly such a significance was later ascribed, the Muratorian writer pointing out that in writing to seven churches Paul was writing to all the church, and Tertullian (*Adv. Marc.* 5. 17) that in speaking to any one church Paul really addressed all the churches. But such a conception belongs to the Catholic movement of the second century; and if it was shared in any degree by the maker or makers of the collection, we must think of them as early "Catholics," aware of the new trend toward union and eager to further it. The fact that Paul had been a polemic figure in his time and was still perhaps often thought of in a merely partisan way would give their enterprise an additional point. Paul, as they saw him, had been an inspired teacher of the entire church, not merely the spokesman for a section of it.

[2] E. J. Goodspeed, *op. cit.,* pp. 51-52; J. Knox, *Philemon Among the Letters of Paul* (Chicago: University of Chicago Press, 1935), p. 51.

In a word, we can hardly fail to see a correspondence between the collection of Paul's letters and the growing consolidation of the churches. The idea of a corpus of letters answers to the developing conception of the church as the body of Christ.

This "catholicizing" purpose of the collection appears more clearly if we can think of the writing of Ephesians in connection with it. For Ephesians is admittedly the most explicitly Catholic document in the New Testament. In its first paragraph its writer affirms that the whole "purpose" of God in Christ was "to unite all things in him, things in heaven and things on earth" (1:10). In other words, the universe as well as humanity is to be "reconciled" in him. The church is the token of this purpose. It is only "through the church" that the "manifold wisdom of God," the "plan of the mystery hidden for ages in God who created all things"—it is only "through the church" that this purpose of God is "made known [even] to the principalities and powers in the heavenly places" (3:9-10).

This reconciling purpose, eventually to comprehend the cosmos, but now manifest in the church, is celebrated in almost every paragraph of this great document. Christ is the "head over all things for the church, which is his body, the fulness of him who fills all in all" (1:22-23). The Gentiles were once "separated from Christ, alienated from the commonwealth of Israel, . . . without God in the world. But now in Christ Jesus . . . [they] have been brought near. . . . For he is our peace, who has made us both one, and has broken down the dividing wall of hostility, . . . that he might create in himself one new man in place of the two [that is, Jew and Greek], . . . and might reconcile us both to God in one body" (2:12-16). Gentiles are now "no longer strangers, . . . but . . . are fellow citizens with the saints and members of the household of God, built upon the foundation of the apostles and prophets, Christ Jesus himself being the chief cornerstone, in whom the whole structure is joined together and grows into a holy temple in the Lord" (2:19-22). All Christians, then, are "fellow heirs, members of the same body, and partakers of the promise" (3:6). They are to forbear "one another in love, eager to maintain the unity of the Spirit in the bond of peace. There is one body and one Spirit, . . . one hope. . ., one Lord, one faith, one baptism, one God and Father of us all, who is above all and through all and in all" (4:2-6). God's gifts of apostles, prophets, evangelists, pastors, and teachers were for the purpose of "building up the body of Christ, until we all attain to the unity of the faith" (4:11-13). Thus, we "are to grow up in every way into him who is the head, into Christ, from whom the whole body, joined and knit together . . . , upbuilds itself in love" (4:15-16). Christ "loved the church and gave himself up for her," is united and identified with her (as in an ideal marriage), "nourishes and cherishes" her as his own "body" (5:25-30).

The word "church," which is generally used by Paul (and other writers) to designate a local congregation,[3] in Ephesians invariably means the whole church, the "Israel of God," the "body of Christ." The fact that this letter alone among the ten in the original collection, or indeed among all the letters attributed to Paul, is addressed to no particular indvidual or church, but to "the saints who are also faithful in Christ Jesus" (1:1)—the fact, in other words, that it is a general letter ad-

[3] See J. Y. Campbell, "The Origin and Meaning of the Christian Use of the Word EKKΛHΣIA," *Journal of Theological Studies*, XLIX (1930), 130-42. In this important essay Professor Campbell argues with impressive evidence that there is no adequate ground for regarding the term ἐκκλησία as having a primarily corporate meaning either in the Septuagint or in the New Testament. He is not disputing the existence of a corporate consciousness, whether in Israel or in the church, but the use of this term to designate it.

dressed to the whole church—is in line with its total and consistent character as a "Catholic" document.

If Paul was really the author of Ephesians, then he was more of a "Catholic" than the other letters would indicate (although it can be argued that Ephesians only develops what is implicit in indisputable writings of the apostle). It seems more likely, however, that this document belongs to the end of the first century and reflects the actual beginnings of the Catholic movement.[4] Since this was the period when the letters of Paul were collected and since it is certain that Ephesians belonged to that collection from the start, it has been proposed that the epistle was written in close connection with the collection. "It has not been settled," writes J. Weiss, "whether the author of the Epistle to the Ephesians is not the same person as the collector of the Pauline corpus. Certainly his spirit, perhaps also his hand, makes itself perceptible." [5] This suggestion of connection, if not identity, between the author of Ephesians and the collector is strengthened by Dr. Goodspeed's demonstration (confirmed in essentials by C. L. Mitton's independent work) that the author knew the other letters and drew largely on this knowledge. Dr. Goodspeed

---

[4] We obviously do not have opportunity here to discuss the highly controversial issue of the authorship of Ephesians. For excellent presentations of the case which conclude against authorship by Paul see J. Weiss, *The History of Primitive Christianity*, II, 682 ff.; E. J. Goodspeed, *The Meaning of Ephesians* (Chicago: University of Chicago Press, 1933), pp. 3-75; James Moffatt, *Introduction to the Literature of the New Testament* (New York: Chas. Scribner's Sons, 1911), pp. 373-85; F. W. Beare, "The Epistle to the Ephesians," *The Interpreter's Bible*, X, 597-607; C. L. Mitton, *The Epistle to the Ephesians* (Oxford: Oxford University Press, 1951). The traditional position is supported by T. Zahn, *Introduction to the New Testament* (Edinburgh: T. & T. Clark, 1909); E. F. Scott, *The Literature of the New Testament* (New York: Columbia University Press, 1932); and, most recently and exhaustively, by Ernst Percy, *Die Probleme der Kolosser- und Epheserbriefe* (Lund: G. W. K. Gleerup, 1946).

[5] *Op. cit.* II, 684.

argues that Ephesians (without the later church name, of course) was the opening or prefatory letter of the corpus, the letter to all the church which was designed to introduce the collection of letters written originally and severally to separate churches. Dr. Goodspeed writes:

Without some fine covering message of harmony and rconciliation those letters, some of which were veritable firebrands of controversy, might actually do more harm than good. It is the greatness of Ephesians that it supplied that irenic interpretation and, by putting it in the mouth of Paul himself, threw the whole Pauline literature into step with the close of the century, when discord was the thing most to be feared, and the call to unity was what the churches most needed. The word "unity" first occurs, in Christian literature, in Ephesians.[6]

[6] *New Solutions of New Testament Problems,* p. 15. See also *The Meaning of Ephesians.* Some support, I venture to say, has been given to his proposal about the primacy of Ephesians in the collection by some suggestions of my own as to the connection of Philemon with the collection and as to the original order of the epistles of Paul. See *Philemon Among the Letters of Paul* and *Marcion and the New Testament* (Chicago: University of Chicago Press, 1942) , pp. 39-76.

It is a very striking fact that the same collection, but with Galatians in first place, was the principal document of the most vigorous partisan movement of the second century, the great Marcionite heresy. It is attractive to surmise that it was Marcion who first collected Paul's letters—so W. Bauer seems to think (*Rechtgläubigkeit und Ketzerei im ältesten Christentum* [Tübingen: J. C. B. Mohr, 1934], p. 224) —and that the first corpus was therefore not the Catholic but the partisan corpus. In that event, we should need to think of Ephesians as replacing Galatians at the head of the corpus when the collection was "catholicized." It is much more likely, however, that the Catholic corpus was the earlier. To the reasons for this view which I have summarized in *Marcion and the New Testament,* pp. 172 ff., I would add the following: (1) If the original corpus was Marcion's with Galatians in first place, it is hard to understand the inclusion of Ephesians at all unless Ephesians is to be thought of as a genuine letter of Paul's, which on other grounds seems unlikely; certainly, all will agree, Ephesians was not produced under Marcionite auspices. (2) If we get past this difficulty and decide that Ephesians might have belonged to an original Marcionite corpus, it is hard to understand the fact that it is, according to length, at the wrong place in

It is perhaps worth pointing out that the case for regarding Ephesians as the first letter in the corpus does not fall or stand with the case for or against the Pauline authorship. Even if Paul's thought had proceeded further in the Catholic direction than most scholars suppose and the Letter to the Ephesians, despite acknowledged peculiarities in style and content, was written by him—even so, it is most natural to conclude that it occupied first place in the collected letters. This is true because of the nonlocal or general character of its address. The collection was a collection of letters to churches, and, if we can judge by all the later lists, the titles of the several sections were "To the Corinthians," "To the Romans," and the like. Where could a letter without a particular address, a letter obviously intended for a general audience, be placed in such a collection? Where, except at the beginning? This is as true if Paul wrote it as if he did not. The conclusion requires as a basis only the two obvious facts: first, that some one letter must in the nature of the case have stood first in the collection, and secondly, that Ephesians was the one general letter in the collection—proclaimed such not by the textual facts alone, but by its whole substance and character. The view, then, that Ephesians probably headed the original corpus does not necessarily presuppose the pseudonymity of the epistle; that position for it is likely in any case. But if it had first place, it would have clarified and confirmed the "Catholic" implications of the collection itself.

In a word, the whole corpus headed by Ephesians (whatever one's views of the origin of that document alone) must be seen not only as a product of the growing Catholic movement, but also as a powerful instrument for its use. Paul, who had been

the order of his list, following Thessalonians when its length would seem to require that it precede those letters.

108

a highly controversial figure and some of whose letters bore such unmistakable traces of bitter conflict, emerges as an ecumenical leader concerned deeply for the unity of the church. This picture, as we were seeing in the preceding chapter, does not convey a false impression. It conveys just the impression his letters as a whole would make on any reader, ancient or modern. But it is not the impression several of his letters taken alone would have made; and it is more than likely that at the end of the century partisan use was being made of some of the more polemic parts of Paul's correspondence. The collection with the addition of Ephesians restores the true balance and throws the weight and strength of Paul the great apostle to the Gentiles into the growing effort to unify the church.

II

That such an effort was being made at the end of the century almost all the later books of the New Testament, not to mention the Apostolic Fathers, provide abundant witness. The ground is familiar, but a quick survey of it may not be out of place.

As we have seen, the Synoptic Gospels, and even more clearly the Fourth, reflect concern for unity. We cannot know to what extent this concern provided the motivation for the writing of the several Gospels. It is fair to assume that part at least of the purpose of such a Gospel as Matthew was the production of a work that would displace several earlier and possibly regional accounts of Jesus' life and teaching, thus contributing to the unity of the church. Certainly, as things worked out, this Gospel (the most widely used of all in the ancient church) had this effect. Luke almost says as much as this about the purpose of his Gospel (as well as of Acts) in his preface (Luke 1:1-4). The Gospel of Matthew is especially rich in signs of concern about the consolidation and the order of the church. The teachings of

Jesus are apparently arranged for catechetical instruction and are thought of as a new Torah. The word "church," appearing twice in Matthew and nowhere else in the Gospels, once refers to a local congregation (18:17), but once to the church universal (16:18). Whatever one makes of the assertion that Christ will build his church upon "this rock"—and I can see no sufficient reason for not regarding it as a reference to Peter himself [7]—or of the allusion to the power of binding and loosing in that same connection, it is clear that Matthew thought of the church throughout the world as a "visible" society with an order and discipline instituted by Christ himself. Concern with unity is hardly less conspicuous in the Fourth Gospel, with its pervasive church-consciousness, its emphasis upon *agape*, its promise of "one flock" and "one shepherd" (10:16), its validation of the disciples as Christ's chosen representatives (6:70; 17:18), and the great prayer of Christ "not . . . for these only, but also for those who are to believe in me through their word, that they may all be one."

We have observed Paul's acknowledgment of the authority of the apostle and his insistence upon the importance of that authority to the order and unity of the church. It is interesting to note how clearly, repeatedly, and emphatically the Gospels strike this same note. One is likely to think first of such texts as "I will give you the keys of the kingdom of heaven . . ." (Matt. 16:19) or "Whatever you bind on earth shall be bound in heaven, and whatever you loose on earth shall be loosed in heaven" (Matt. 18:18; compare John 20:20-23). But to passages of this kind must be added the several in which the authority vested in the disciples is referred to in connection with Jesus' choice and

<hr/>

[7] So O. Cullmann, *Peter*, tr. F. V. Filson (Philadelphia: Westminster Press, 1953) pp. 206-7; but I should say that the words represent the thought of some part of the early church, rather than Jesus' own conception.

commissioning of them, as, for example, "He . . . sent [them] out to preach and have authority to cast out demons" (Mark 3: 14-15; compare Mark 6:7; Matt. 9:37-10:2; Luke 6:12-13; 9: 1-2, 6; John 6:70; 15:16). Equally impressive are the directions Jesus gives his disciples when he sends them out (see Matt. 10:5-15 and Luke 10:2-12), culminating in such sweeping assurances as "He who receives you receives me, and he who receives me receives him who sent me" (Matt. 10:40), or "He who hears you hears me, and he who rejects you rejects me, and he who rejects me rejects him who sent me" (Luke 10:16), or (in a somewhat different context) "As thou didst send me into the world, so I have sent them into the world" (John 17:18; compare 13: 18-20). Controversy as to whether all, or any, of these passages go back to Jesus in the flesh has obscured the fact that, whether they do or not, they reflect a common and very primitive understanding on the part of the early church; and *this,* for our present purpose, is the important thing.

It can be argued that for Jesus his disciples constituted, not officials of the church, but the community itself; and that such words of his as have just been quoted were intended to confer authority on the whole church, not on the apostles as such. The whole church was "sent."[8] But it is much easier to make this point about Jesus' original intention (assuming the authenticity of the words themselves) than about the way the words were understood in the primitive church; and we must keep in mind that it is this understanding with which we are at present really concerned. Could Luke 22:28-30 (compare Matt. 19:28), "You are those who have continued with me in my trials; as my Father appointed a kingdom for me, so do I appoint for you that you

---

[8] See in this connection T. W. Manson's important book *The Church's Ministry* (Philadelphia: Westminster Press, 1948).

may eat and drink at my table in my kingdom, and sit on thrones judging the twelve tribes of Israel"—could such a passage have been understood, say in A.D. 80, as not being addressed to the twelve apostles in their official capacity?

It is not unlikely, to be sure, that the very emphasis which the Gospels all place upon the authority of the apostles (especially the later Gospels) indicates that in the latter years of the first century that authority was being disputed. But would it have been the authority of the *apostles* that was in dispute, or the authority of contemporary church officials who were regarded—or at least regarded themselves—as in some sense their successors? In other words, do we not have in the very emphasis upon apostolic authority *at a time when none of the apostles would have been alive* an evidence that some conception of succession was already in existence?

Concerning Luke-Acts, and especially the Acts section, I have already spoken at some length.[9] No one will question that its way of telling the story of primitive Christianity is affected in every part by its interest in promoting the unity of the contemporary church. Christians everywhere belong to the true Israel, the covenant people of God. To set forth this character of Christianity as successor to, indeed the continuation of, the Hebrew-Jewish religious community (and therefore a corporate unity) is perhaps the primary objective of Luke-Acts. We have interpreted Ephesians and the first Pauline letter collection as being, under one aspect at least, an effort to present Paul as an ecumenical church leader; Acts might be described, also under one aspect, as another effort of the same kind. In the collected letters Paul is allowed to speak for himself, for the most part; in Acts an interpreter speaks for him. But in both cases Paul

[9] See pp. 30-34.

speaks to the whole church and for the sake of the whole church. The author of Acts does his best to present a convincing picture of an early church at peace with itself, united in a common order and gladly acknowledging the authority of the Jerusalem authorities, whether "the apostles and the elders" (15:6) or "James . . . and all the elders" (21:18). One does not need to doubt his sincerity in order to recognize that he would probably not have presented the primitive situation just as he did, or indeed have seen it so, if he had not been concerned to help unify and consolidate the church in his own time.

It is not too much to say that this interest entirely dominates the Pastoral epistles, with their insistence upon a sound doctrine and a well-ordered polity. The very existence of general or "catholic" epistles—whether addressed (formally at least) to the whole church or to a large section of it—reveals a consciousness of the church universal and a desire to strengthen its corporate character. First Peter sees the church as "a holy nation, God's own people" (2:9) and speaks of the "brotherhood throughout the world" (5:9). The Johannine epistles as a whole (like the Gospel) emphasize *agape* as a special bond of union among Christians (separating them from the world as certainly as it makes them one), and reveal a keen interest both in the defining and consolidating of the church's faith and (especially in Third John) in the maintaining of a sound polity. The Epistle to the Hebrews, it would appear, besides calling for submission to responsible leaders (13:17; compare 1 Peter 5:1-3), all but challenges the Roman church to become the teacher of the churches (Heb. 5:12). The book of Revelation is as much an appeal for unity among the churches of Asia as for loyalty, and, moreover, implies some kind of acknowledged authority on the part of its author. First Clement we have already noted in discussing Paul's

113

correspondence with Corinth.[10] Troubled by the continuing, or recurring, anarchy within the Corinthian church, its author finds in the Old Testament priesthood a type of the church's ministry (40:5) and, first among Christian writers, refers to the bishops (elders) as successors to the apostles (44:1-3). The letters of Ignatius are full of concern for ecclesiastical order, particularly for the establishment of monepiscopacy among all the churches. And one may see in the very act of collecting the letters of Ignatius (as in the earlier collecting of Paul's letters) an indication of the developing Catholic consciousness. The Epistle of Polycarp is preoccupied with issues of unity and order. In a word, few if any of the Christian documents written around the end of the first century can be understood apart from the strong movement toward consolidation which was manifesting itself in every part of the church.

III

The evidence of Irenaeus, Tertullian, and others puts it beyond dispute that a century later this movement was far advanced and that by A.D. 200 what is known as the early Catholic church was fully in existence, a church conscious of itself as being *the* church—one, universal, and apostolic. As to the steps in the process by which this end was reached, the evidence is much less sure and clear, and at many points no certainty is possible. Presentations of early Catholicism usually focus attention on its achievement of agreement as regards canon, creed, and episcopacy; and the rest of our own brief discussion may appropriately center around these three topics. My concern at each point will be to show that although the situation of A.D. 200 did not exist in New Testament times, there were pointers in its

[10] See p. 35.

direction; that the several features of Catholicism cannot be understood simply as *ad hoc* responses to the threats of Gnostic heresy and the state's hostility, but were anticipated in, and in a degree fulfillments of, tendencies already present in the New Testament church.

Consider first the case of the canon.[11] There is no evidence of the existence of what we know as the New Testament, a second sacred collection of writings comparable in authority with the inherited Hebrew-Jewish Scriptures, until the time of Irenaeus, rather late in the second century. Even Irenaeus does not use the term "New Testament," but he manifestly is familiar with the thing itself. The contents of the New Testament that he accepted were destined to be altered in details in subsequent developments, until the final New Testament, our own canon, was established at the end of the fourth century; but the structure and substance of the new canon had already been determined in Irenaeus' time. The Muratorian fragment, Tertullian, and Clement of Alexandria are additional witnesses to its existence. But Justin, less than half a century earlier, does not know of it and must carry on his apologetic and polemic work without its help.

Now there can be little doubt that the formation of the New Testament was immediately precipitated by the use such heretics as Marcion were making of Christian writings. The canon was an instrument specifically forged to do battle with these second-

[11] One may refer to such well-known histories of the New Testament canon as B. F. Westcott, *A General Survey of the History of the Canon of the New Testament* (London, 1855-70); T. Zahn, *Geschichte des neutestamentlichen Kanons* (Erlangen, 1888); E. J. Goodspeed, *The Formation of the New Testament* (Chicago: University of Chicago Press, 1926); etc. Of great importance for the understanding of the structure of the canon is A. von Harnack, *The Origin of the New Testament* (New York: The Macmillan Co., 1925).

century schismatics. But it is equally certain that the beginnings of the development that would inevitably have led to the creation of the New Testament canon—although probably not in the form we know—lie in the New Testament period. The importance of the memory of Jesus to the early church and the authority his remembered words possessed—factors that had already led to the writing of gospels—would just as surely (as gospels multiplied) have led eventually to the definition of the authoritative Gospel; and this would have been tantamount to canonization. The collection of the letters of Paul is, without intending to be, a prediction, almost a promise, of an ampler and more authoritative apostolic collection. Harnack makes much of the idea of the new covenant in Paul as containing the germ of the new canon.[12] Since there were books of the old covenant (almost explicitly referred to as such in II Cor. 3:14), there were bound to be books of the new covenant when the time was ripe. Marcion undoubtedly hastened the time and also left his unmistakable mark on the product; [13] but the time would have come in any case. It was inevitable that Christians should have sought agreement on what books most immediately reflected and most truly recorded the event to which the church looked back as the source and norm of its own life; and it is not unlikely that, Marcion and the heretics aside, they would eventually have agreed on the books that form the core of our canon. In other words, the New Testament was an inevitable development, although a development that for the greater part lies outside the New Testament period itself.

The same kind of thing can be said about the creed. What

---

[12] *The Origin of the New Testament,* pp. 12-16.

[13] See *Marcion and the New Testament,* pp. 19-38; also E. C. Blackman, *Marcion and His Influence* (London: Society for Promoting Christian Knowledge, 1949), pp. 23-37.

---

we know as the Apostles' Creed did not take its present form till medieval times, but a formulation virtually equivalent to it can be traced as far back as the second century. This formulation, sometimes called the Old Roman Symbol, originally a brief elaboration of the trinitarian formula, was enlarged under the influence of the Gnostic controversy so as to affirm belief in "God, the Father Almighty"; in "Christ Jesus, the Son of God, who was born of the Holy Ghost of the Virgin Mary, and was crucified under Pontius Pilate, and was dead and buried, and rose again the third day, alive from the dead, and ascended into heaven, and sat at the right hand of the Father, and will come to judge the quick and the dead"; and in "the Holy Ghost, and the holy church, and the resurrection of the flesh." This reconstruction is based on Hippolytus (*Apos. Trad.* 21. 12-17); [14] but very similar forms of confession are found in Irenaeus (*Adv. Haer.* 1. 10. 1) and in his contemporary Tertullian (*De Praesc. Haeret.* 13), not to mention such apocryphal works as the Acts of Paul and the Epistle of the Apostles.[15] Together they establish the existence by A.D. 200 of a commonly accepted definition of faith substantially identical with the later Apostles' Creed. The Nicene Creed was, of course, an elaboration of this same definition.

Now although this old Roman creed was generally ascribed

[14] See the text in B. S. Easton, tr., *The Apostolic Tradition of Hippolytus* (Cambridge: Cambridge University Press, 1934), pp. 46-47. See also Gregory Dix, *The Shape of the Liturgy* (London: The Dacre Press, 1945), p. 485. For various other attempts to reconstruct this second-century creed see A. C. McGiffert, *The Apostles Creed: Its Origin, Its Purpose and Its Historical Interpretation* (New York: Chas. Scribner's Sons, 1902), p. 100; H. Lietzmann in *Festgabe für Adolf von Harnack* (Tübingen: J. C. B. Mohr, 1921), pp. 226 ff.; and K. Holl, *Gesammelte Aufsälze zur Kirchengeschichte* (Tübingen: J. C. B. Mohr, 1928), II, 115 ff.

[15] For a very convenient bringing together of much of this material, with suggestive comment, see M. Rist, "Pseudepigraphical Refutations of Marcionism," *Journal of Religion*, XXII (1942), 39-50.

to the apostles—Tertullian can attribute a somewhat expanded form of it to Jesus himself!—it does not require much critical acumen to see the marks of its second-century origin. The Apostles' Creed, or any equivalent of it, simply cannot be dated in the times of the apostles. And yet one cannot miss the first-century pointers in its direction. Cullmann and others have called attention to the need of confessional formulas in the New Testament period—in connection with baptism, in regular worship, in exorcisms, when one was challenged to make one's defense in persecutions, and the like—and have cited the traces of such confessional formulas in the New Testament itself.[16] At an earlier stage in this discussion I ventured to speak of the "first Christian creed" as the confession of Jesus as Lord and Christ, and then I went on to show both that this confession was inescapably implied in the very life of the church and also that it was itself rich in implications as to the directions further developments of the doctrine of Christ might and might not take.[17] Given the particular heretical challenge of the second century, something like the Apostles' Creed was an inevitable development; and one might almost say that the heresies themselves were predetermined, since they *were* heresies only because they were denials of what had been established as essential in the primitive memory (Jesus), the primitive corporate experience (the Lord, the Spirit, the church), and the primitive faith (the Christ of God). These essentials had been firmly established in the New Testament period, and they determined in advance what future variations

[16] O. Cullmann, *Les premières confessions de foi Chrétiennes* (Paris: Presses Universitaires de France, 1948). See also E. Stauffer, *Die Theologie des Neuen Testaments* (Stuttgart: Kohlhammer, 1945), pp. 212-34; C. H. Dodd, *The Apostolic Preaching and Its Developments* (London: Hodder & Stoughton, Ltd., 1936); and J. N. D. Kelly, *Early Christian Creeds* (London and New York: Longmans, Green & Co., 1950), especially pp. 7-29.

[17] See pp. 68-82.

of belief could be absorbed, or at least tolerated, and what would have to be rejected as heretical aberration and distortion. In a word, the creed, like the canon, cannot be traced earlier than the middle of the second century, but the promise of it, and the essential substance of it, can be clearly discerned in the first.

As for episcopacy, one hesitates to venture into so hotly contested a field,[18] but I suggest that the same kind of double statement can be made about it too. Monarchical episcocacy is, generally speaking, a second-century development; but although it is impossible to work out with certainty or in any detail the con-

[18] In the current discussion important titles are Kirk, ed., *The Apostolic Ministry* (London: Hodder & Stoughton, Ltd., 1946) ; T. W. Manson, *The Church's Ministry* (Philadelphia: Westminster Press, 1948) ; C. C. Richardson, *The Sacrament of Reunion* (New York: Chas. Scribner's Sons, 1940) , pp. 34-74; T. O. Wedel, *The Coming Great Church* (New York: The Macmillan Co., 1945) , especially pp. 80-158; W. D. Davies, *A Normative Pattern of Church Life in the New Testament: Fact or Fancy?* (London: James Clarke & Co., 1950) ; C. F. D. Moule and H. Chadwick in *The Office of a Bishop* (London: Church Book Room Press, 1948) ; R. R. Williams, *Authority in the Apostolic Age* (London: S. C. M. Press, 1950) , especially pp. 42-74; James Gray, "Authority of Scripture and Tradition," *Shane Quarterly*, XIV (1953) , 59-85; O. Linton, "Church and Office in the New Testament" in A. Nygren *et al.*, eds., *This Is the Church* (Philadelphia: Muhlenberg Press, 1952) ; H. von Campenhausen, *Kirchliches Amt und geistliche Vollmacht in den ersten drei Jahrhunderten* (Tübingen: J. C. B. Mohr, 1953) ; A. Ehrhardt, *The Apostolic Succession* (London: Lutterworth Press, 1953) ; Kenneth M. Carey, ed., *The Historic Episcopacy in the Fullness of the Church* (London: The Dacre Press, 1954) . Of earlier works on the general subject of the polity of the primitive church one may cite: E. Hatch, *The Organization of the Early Christian Churches* (Oxford and Cambridge, 1881) ; J. B. Lightfoot, "The Christian Ministry," in *St. Paul's Epistle to the Philippians* (London: Macmillan & Co., 1890) , pp. 179-267; F. J. A. Hort, *The Christian Ecclesia* (London: Macmillan & Co., 1897) ; W. Lowrie, *The Church and Its Organization* (New York: Longmans, Green & Co., 1904) ; A. von Harnack, *The Constitution and Law of the Church in the First Two Centuries* (New York: G. P. Putnam, 1911)) ; H. Lietzmann, "Zur altchristlichen Verfassungsgeschichte," *Zeitschrift für wissenschaftliche Theologie*, LV (1914) , 97-153; B. H. Streeter, *The Primitive Church* (New York: The Macmillan Co., 1929) ; O. Linton, *Das Problem der Urkirche in der neueren Forschung* (Uppsala: Lundequistska, 1932) ; K. L. Schmidt, "Le Ministère et les ministères dans l'église du Nouveau Testament," *Revue d'Histoire et de Philosophie religieuse*, XVII (1937) , 313-36; B. S. Easton, *The Pastoral Epistles* (New York: Chas. Scribner's Sons, 1947) .

nections between the bishops of the second century and the apostles of the first, still the institution of episcopacy does represent a true and all but inevitable sequel to the apostolic office and function.

There can be little doubt that by the end of the second century most, if not all, of the churches, although they may also have had their bodies of elders, were ruled primarily by single bishops, who exercised superior liturgical, teaching, disciplinary, and administrative powers. As to the stages by which this situation was arrived at, our meager sources leave us in great uncertainty. Although Paul refers to bishops in Phil. 1:1, as does First Clement in 42:4, neither does so in a way to suggest the monarchical episcopate. The bishops are referred to in the plural and, in both cases, in connection with deacons. There are many additional indications that in a large part of the church, in the first century and early in the second, congregations were ruled by councils of presbyters (i.e., elders), who might also be called bishops (i.e., rulers or overseers). This would seem to be the picture emerging in the Pastoral epistles, where the two terms "presbyter" and "bishop" are apparently used interchangeably.[19] The reason for the variety in terminology is probably, at least in part, linguistic. The idea of government by councils of elders was taken over from Judaism; but when Christianity moved into Gentile communities where the term "elder" was unfamiliar as a title of office, these officials tended to be called by the more congenial term "ruler" or "bishop." [20] Such councils of

[19] But this statement would be challenged by many, who hold that while all bishops were presbyters, not all presbyters were bishops. But see I Tim. 3:2 ff.; 5:17 ff.; Tit. 1:5-9; I Clem. 44:4-6; 47:6; 54:2.

[20] So B. S. Easton, *The Pastoral Epistles*, pp. 189-90; but in *The Apostolic Tradition of Hippolytus*, pp. 80-81, Easton seems to be offering a somewhat different suggestion: "In the Pastoral Epistles and I Clement, 'presbyters' are divided into 'bishops' and 'deacons'—in these works the three terms

presbyter-bishops appear everywhere in the book of Acts,[21] and would seem to have been the first widely prevalent type of church order in the post-apostolic age. Unlike the Jewish elders, they had priestly, as well as administrative, responsibilities and powers, being charged with officiating at the Eucharist. We do not know how early the presbyters began to be called "priests," but there is good reason to believe the term was being generally applied by the end of the second century.[22]

Meantime, however, another type of church order had been emerging. It is clear that even as early as Paul's time James the brother of Jesus had a certain pre-eminence among the presbyters at Jersualem; [23] and the letters of Ignatius put beyond question that early in the second century monarchical episcopacy in the full sense prevailed in Antioch, Ignatius' own church, and in the churches of Asia. Even these letters, however, give some indication that this situation had not at that time become universal, because in writing to the Romans, Ignatius says nothing of their "bishop," although very great attention has been paid to the bishops of the other churches. The same meaning can be

---

are never used together—indicating specializations within the presbyterate. Some presbyters were especially concerned with 'overseeing' the community and others with 'serving' it." Lietzmann (*op. cit.*, pp. 108 ff.) regards "elders," found in some churches, as being the general body of the rulers or leaders of the congregation which, in other churches, is broken down into "prophets," "teachers," "bishops," and "deacons," This kind of discrimination, or classification, appears, he argues, in the Didache and also in Paul, whose "helpers and administrators" (ἀντιλήμψεις, κυβερνήσεις) in I Cor. 12:28 are regarded as identical with the "deacons" and "bishops" of Phil. 1:1.

[21] Acts 11:30; 14:23; 15:2, 4, 6, 22, 23; 16:4; 20:17 (cf. 20:28). Cf. I Pet. 5:1-2; James 5:14.

[22] See I Clem. 40:5; 44:4: Did. 13:3; Ign. Phila. 4; Tertullian *On Baptism* 17: *Exhortation to Chastity* 7, 11; Hippolytus *Apos. Trad.* 9:2 See also Barton Le Roy Burkhart, "The Rise of the Christian Priesthood,' an unpublished Ph.D. dissertation (University of Chicago, 1938).

[23] Gal. 2:9; cf. Acts 21:18 ff.

121

seen in Polycarp's reference (5:3) to the "elders and deacons" at Philippi, rather than to the "bishops and deacons" mentioned in Paul's letter to the same church (1:1). Polycarp is
himself bishop of Smyrna (he is so called in Ign. Poly. 1:1
and Magn. 15:1) and begins his own letter to the Philippians,
"Polycarp and the elders with him . . ."; but Philippi apparently
does not have a bishop in the exclusive sense, and if rulers of the
church there have to be addressed in the plural, he prefers "elders"
to "bishops." [24]

We have, then, at the beginning of the second century a situation in which the majority of churches are apparently governed by
boards of elders, but in which a considerable number have accepted the monarchical-bishop pattern. It is perhaps not an
accident that these latter churches seem to have lain in the more
eastern part of the church—specifically, Antioch [25] and the
churches of Asia. Just as the "elder" system, adopted from
Judaism, was probably first established in Palestine, so it is not
unlikely that James's pre-eminence at Jerusalem suggested the
plan of a single ruler to the churches farther west.[26] But what-

[24] So, among others, H. von Campenhausen, *Kirchliches Amt und geistliche
Vollmacht in den ersten drei Jahrhunderten*, p. 130. Campenhausen argues
that Polycarp's opening words mean that he places himself on an equality
with the "elders with him" and that he did not see himself as Ignatius saw
him.

[25] But the Didache and possibly Matt. 18:15-17 and 23:8-10 indicate that
not all Syrian churches had followed Antioch. On the other hand, Ignatius
calls himself "bishop of Syria" (Ign. Rom. 2:2; cf. 9:1). Questions of date and
provenance for the Didache and of source analysis for Matthew complicate
the issue. Harnack sees evidence in Ign. Phila. 10 that there were other
bishops in Syria in this period and explains the title "bishop of Syria" by
Antioch's metropolitan position (*Mission and Expansion of Christianity*
[New York: G. P. Putnam's Sons, 1908], I, 463).

[26] See B. S. Easton, *The Pastoral Epistles*, p. 227. See also W. K. L. Clarke,
"The Origins of Episcopacy" in Jenkins and Mackenzie, eds., *Episcopacy,
Ancient and Modern* (London: Society for Promoting Christian Knowledge,
1930), pp. 2 ff.

ever the direction of the movement—or whether it had a "direction" at all—there is no question that it gradually, and fairly rapidly, prevailed, and that by the time of Irenaeus and Tertullian it was generally established. It would appear that, except possibly for Egypt, every important church at the beginning of the third century had its bishop.

Now this result would seem to have been the consequence— inevitable as things were—of the operation of two factors, one pressing from the bottom, so to speak, and the other from the top. As the source of the pressure "from the bottom" I mean the conviction of the congregations severally, growing out of actual experience, that a single head was needed not only for the efficient administration of the work of the church, constantly increasing in scope and complexity, but also for the proper carrying out of its liturgical, teaching, and pastoral functions. As the elder system proved too cumbersome, one of the elders would naturally be recognized as the leading elder and would eventually become the bishop in the monarchical sense. Presumably at the beginning it would have been the congregations or the local boards of elders who chose and appointed the bishops.[27] Often a prophetic leader would have emerged, and the congregation or elders would have appeared to be only acknowledging God's own choice for the office.

Especially important among the functions of this bishop (or principal elder) was that of presiding at the Eucharist. Many indeed see the rise of monepiscopacy primarily in the context of early Christian liturgical practice. The office of presiding at

[27] In the early *Apostolic Tradition* of Hippolytus (not long after A.D. 200) we read: "Let the bishop be ordained after he has been chosen by all the people. When he has been named and shall please all, let him, with the presbytery and such bishops as may be present, assemble with the people on a Sunday. When all give their consent, the bishops shall lay their hands upon him, and the presbytery shall stand by in silence" (2:1-3). Cf. I Clem. 44:3.

the Lord's Supper, which was the central act of the congregation's worship from the very beginning, gradually took on other prerogatives and became the later bishop's office. In the description by Justin Martyr of early Christian worship at Rome near the middle of the second century minor references are made to "deacons" and to a "reader," but the important cult official is apparently the "president"; [28] and he is mentioned most prominently in connection with the administration of the Eucharist. This "president" may well be the official elsewhere called "bishop." With greater certainty we can identify the bishop in the Ignatian epistles as being primarily the guardian and guarantor of the communion table.[29] The sacerdotal significance we have noted as belonging very early to the council of presbyters would be thus focused in the bishop's office.

But whatever the monarchical bishop's primary function may have been, it is possible to understand the office as the creation of the local church, through the elevation of one of the elders, for the purpose of giving unity and direction to its life and work. And when a congregation was divided to make several, or new churches were formed under its influence and in its environment, the bishop would stand in a supervisory relation to them all. Many explain the rise of diocesan episcopacy in this way; certainly it must be partly thus explained.

But another explanation of this development is available in what I have called a "pressure from the top." We have observed

---

[28] *Apol.* I, 67 (cf. 65). The word προεστώς may refer to a temporary presiding officer; but a permanent official seems much more likely.

[29] See, e.g., Ign. Smyrn. 8; Trall. 2; Phila. 4. Also W. Lowrie, *op. cit.*, pp. 266-313; A. E. J. Rawlinson, "The Historical Origin of the Christian Ministry," in *Foundations* (London: Macmillan & Co., 1914), pp. 408-22; T. O. Wedel, *op. cit.*, pp. 139-42; and M. H. Shepherd, "The Development of the Early Ministry," *Anglican Theological Review*, XXVI (1944), 135 ff.

that even from the beginning the apostle was recognized as hav-ing, under Christ, supreme authority in the church. We have seen that Paul regards himself as having this authority in the area around the Aegean Sea in which his churches lay, and his claims were apparently acknowledged by the Jerusalem leaders (Gal. 2:1-10).[30] When Paul left this area to go to Jerusalem, and then to Rome and Spain (Rom. 15:23 ff.), he presumably named some deputy, or deputies, to take his place. Whether this oc-curred or not, it would be almost inevitable that when Paul, for whatever reason, ceased to exercise effective direction of his churches, that direction should be taken over by another, or (more probably) by several others, the large territory being di-vided among them. Such persons would most naturally be former associates of Paul and, whether formally ordained by him or not, would stand in quite literal succession to him. We may believe that Onesimus, for example, known to have been bishop of Ephesus around A.D. 115, was one of these.[31] Such a one would be more than a bishop of a local church, presiding over a board of elders; he would be a bishop in what has proved to be the continuing meaning of the term, the overseer of a number of churches in an area or "diocese."

Such an office seems to be presupposed in the Johannine epis-

[30] Possibly in a wider area; see footnote 15 in chapter IV.

[31] In my *Philemon Among the Letters of Paul* I have offered reasons for identifying the Onesimus of Paul's Letter to Philemon and the Onesimus referred to as bishop of Ephesus by Ignatius in his letter to the Ephesians (1:3). I have no way of knowing to what extent the argument has proved convincing. It is favorably regarded by Dr. E. J. Goodspeed and by Dr. A. E. Barnett in their introductions; and by Dr. P. N. Harrison in his "Onesimus and Philemon" in the *Anglican Theological Review* XXXII (1950), 268 ff. If this identification is sound, it has a bearing upon the early history of the episcopate which, I think, has not been taken properly into account. The evidence for this particular instance of succession from an apostle is earlier and, I should say, firmer than for any other case.

tles. The author of these letters is called "the elder," but he obviously has supervision of a number of churches. In Third John he writes to Gaius in protest against the insubordination of a certain Diotrephes, who has apparently assumed a kind of monarchical authority in some local church within the "elder's" area. Many interpreters [32] regard this protest as a protest against the new episcopal system in local church government which was then emerging; but the elder may be objecting only to the identity of this particular incumbent of the bishop's office. In either case, however, the author of the epistles appears as a superintendent of churches.

Similarly, "Timothy" and "Titus," to whom the Pastoral epistles are addressed, are clearly overseers of churches. It is explicitly said that "Titus" is to appoint "elders" in "every town" (Tit. 1:5). "Timothy" and "Titus" themselves are not called "bishops"; but in them, as Easton says, "the Ignatian bishops are actually found in everything but title." [33] Easton points out, however, that the fact of "Timothy's" ordination by elders [34] rather than by other bishops (as in Hippolytus and later) indicates that "the distinction between 'Timothy' and the other elders was one of 'office' and not of 'order,'" adding that "the same may very well be true of the Ignatian bishops as well, for nothing is told of the manner of their ordination." [35]

Streeter is cited as saying that the church had an archbishop before it had a bishop! [36] But this only means that the office of

[32] For example, B. S. Easton, *The Abingdon Bible Commentary* (New York and Nashville: Abingdon Press, 1929), p. 1359. But see also C. H. Dodd, *The Johannine Epistles* (New York: Harper & Bros., 1946), pp. 161-66.

[33] *The Pastoral Epistles*, p. 177.

[34] I Tim. 4:14; II Tim. 1:6, according to Easton, must not be understood as contradicting the other passage.

[35] *Ibid.*, p. 178.

[36] By R. R. Williams (*Authority in the Apostolic Age* [London: S. C. M. Press, 1950], p. 65), referring possibly to *The Primitive Church*, p. 92.

diocesan oversight by a single individual—like "Timothy" or "Titus" or "the elder"—seems to have existed before local churches generally had their own single rulers. The term "bishop" in the exclusive sense was not in the beginning used to designate the regional superintendents; it was first applied to the congregational rulers when they emerged—to men like Diotrephes— probably because the word had traditionally been associated with the government of a local church. Just how the movements "from the bottom" and "from the top" met in the institution of episcopacy conceived of as having apostolic authority, the bishops standing in succession to one another and ultimately to the apostles, we do not know.[37] Indeed, it is certain that no single line of development lies back of the second-century epis- copacy. Ignatius' bishops would seem to be local rulers; but he can call himself, as we have seen, bishop of Syria—which must mean, at least, that as bishop of Antioch, the great city of Syria and one of the first centers of the Christian mission, he held a po- sition of predominating influence in that area. Surely one is not mistaken in seeing a connection of some kind between the primi- tive apostles and such metropolitan bishops.

To say this does not mean agreeing that lines of formal ordina- tions in all cases join the apostles with the bishops, much less that there is any chance of our being able to trace them. It does not require us to affirm that the bishops inherited, or could inherit, the unique and inalienable qualifications of the apostles. It cer- tainly does not involve our subscribing to any theory which holds that the very essence of the church's reality inheres in, or can be conveyed only through, the bishop's office. It does mean

[37] "When we have explained how the supreme powers of the general ministry were made to devolve on individuals who belonged to the local ministry, we have explained the origin of episcopacy" (C. H. Turner in *Cambridge Medieval History*, I, 145, quoted by W. K. L. Clarke, *op. cit.*, p. 39).

our recognizing that a system of government in which oversight of presbyters and even of groups of churches was exercised by some authorized individual was implicit from the start, and that monarchical episcopacy, although a second-century development, was not without antecedents in the first. The factors which produced it were many and complex; and different factors undoubtedly operated in different parts of the church, and in varying degrees of strength. But surely some of its roots lie in the time, early in the New Testament period, when men like Paul and Peter and James began to lay down their tasks of oversight. The monarchical bishops may not have been appointed or authorized by the apostles; but to an extent they filled a vacuum the apostles had left, and in doing so actually inherited some part of their responsibility and authority.

IV

There is something arbitrary, perhaps, in focusing this discussion of early Catholicism upon canon, creed, and ministry. I might have included the developing liturgy of the church, to which such early documents as the Didache and the *Apostolic Tradition* of Hippolytus bear witness and which also had roots in the New Testament period.[38] But more important than recognizing particular omissions of this kind is seeing that all such developments are only phases of the church's effort to realize its true character as a "visible" corporate unity, the body of Christ, God's new Israel, a "holy nation," a "royal priesthood," a "spiritual house" (I Peter 2:5, 9) in which the whole meaning of the revelation in Christ is embodied and the whole of man's need is filled (for the term "Catholic" connotes fullness and adequacy as well as universality and unity). It is not strange that

[38] See again O. Cullmann, *Early Christian Worship* (London: S. C. M. Press, 1953).

this act of self-realization required time. The emergence of Christianity was, under one important aspect, the emergence of a new historical culture; and a culture is not formed in a moment, or in a generation. Jesus and his disciples were at home within the culture of Judaism; and the same can be said, after the Resurrection, of the Palestinian, and perhaps other Jewish, communities. But even then the new wine was stretching the old wineskins; and Judaism soon proved an inadequate home for an essentially universal Spirit. A more appropriate home had to be built—or, rather, had to grow into being. The early Catholics were consciously concerned with the foundations of this building, the beginnings of this growth.

The Catholic movement did not succeed in consolidating the church, as the works of Bauer and Greenslade [39] have reminded us; but it brought the church a larger measure of outward unity than it had had before or than it has had since. The concern of the last two chapters has been to show that early Catholicism cannot be thought of as a mere distortion of primitive Christianity owing to the inevitable loss of some of its original inspiration or to the operation of temporary environmental pressures (although these factors undoubtedly had their effect), but that it was the outworking of tendencies implicit from the beginning. Distortions occurred, to be sure, but Catholicism as such was not a distortion. It was a fulfillment, even if only proximate and quite imperfect, of hopes as old as the church itself. It was the institutional embodying of a corporate consciousness and memory, both innate and essential. It was the culmination of a gradual effort to realize and to express in appropriate forms of polity and cult the unity that belongs to the very nature of the church.

[39] W. Bauer, *Rechtgläubigkeit und Ketzerei im ältesten Christentum* (Tübingen, J. C. B. Mohr, 1934) and S. L. Greenslade, *Schism in the Early Church* (New York: Harper & Bros., 1953).

THE AUTHORITY OF
THE EARLY CHURCH

THUS FAR WE HAVE BEEN TRYING TO AN-
swer a historical question: To what extent and in what sense
was the early church united? In this final chapter we turn to a
question of a quite different kind: To what extent and in what
sense does the early church provide a norm or model for the
united church we all are seeking? What bearing does the experience of primitive Christianity have upon the church's contemporary quest for unity? That this experience is profoundly
relevant and provides us with absolutely indispensable guidance,
all will agree. But can it be relied on alone? Are there limits
to what we are calling the "authority" of the early church?

Although I feel that my task in this book would be left un-
completed if I did not consider this contemporary question, I am
also acutely aware, even more than hitherto, of the narrow limits
of my competence. I write, not as an expert in what has come
to be called "ecumenics," but simply as a Protestant Christian
who has made some study of the early church and is deeply concerned for the great church that is to come.

I

"Holy Scripture containeth all things necessary to salvation:
so that whatsoever is not read therein, nor may be proved thereby,

is not to be required of any man, that it should be believed as an article of the Faith, or be thought requisite or necessary to salvation." So reads the sixth article of the Anglican Thirty-nine Articles of Religion; so in effect reads some one of the articles of faith, explicit or implicit, of every branch of Christendom. The authority of Scripture might be said to be one of the matters on which all Christians are agreed.[1] When we ask, however, precisely how this authority is to be understood, not only is agreement hard to reach, but even satisfactory definition is not easy to attain. It is difficult for any one person or party to say what one really means, much less to say it in a way that wins the assent of others.

Consider, for example, the rather representative statement just quoted.[2] What exactly does it mean? We are told that nothing can be considered essential that cannot be proved by scripture; but does it follow that everything is required that *can* be thus proved? If this is not true, on what basis are we to distinguish between the essential and the nonessential? Again, what does it mean to "read" something in scripture or to "prove" something by scripture? Is a single text found in any part of scripture enough? If so, we must allow that almost everything can be "read therein" or "proved thereby." Or do we mean by what is "read" or may be "proved" a kind of lowest common denominator—teaching common to all the texts? In that case, hardly anything can be identified as essential.

[1] This is true, I should say, of Roman Catholics as well as of others. The authority of tradition, while affirmed and regarded as indispensable, is nevertheless subordinated to the authority of Scripture. Tradition, it is held, is necessary for the true understanding of Scripture.

[2] Compare also the twentieth article, which declares that "it is not lawful for the Church to ordain any thing that is contrary to God's Word written, neither may it so expound one place of Scripture, that it be repugnant to another."

We are undoubtedly moving in the direction of a clearer conception when we recall the relation in which the Scriptures stand to the historical community, Hebrew-Jewish and Christian, and recognize that in speaking of their authority we are really referring to the authority of events within its life and therefore to a certain normativeness in the life itself. The Christian has in mind, more particularly, the "mighty acts" of God in Jesus Christ—the total event which culminated in the creation of the Christian community. Early Christianity, as we have seen,[3] is in a unique sense normative and authoritative Christianity because it stands in a unique relation to this event. The Old Testament has authority because it records and reflects the history which that event presupposes and apart from which it could not have occurred. The New Testament has authority because it recounts and reflects the event itself, including of course the concrete meaning it had within the primitive community. The authority of scripture is the authority of the memory and the Spirit of Christ as these are expressed and embodied in the early church, which claimed and reinterpreted the Old Testament and produced the documents of the New.

But although such a formulation clarifies the situation to a degree, it by no means disposes of all our problems. One finds oneself asking such questions as these: Do elements of faith and practice need to be universal among the primitive churches in order to have authority? If not, how are we to distinguish the normative elements? Do elements emerging only in the latter part of the early period have the same authority as elements present in the very beginning? Does the authority belong only to what can properly be called primitive Christianity—by which phrase we mean, I suppose, the Christianity that produced the

[3] See p. 18.

New Testament documents—or do certain later developments also possess it in some degree?

II

We may make a beginning at discussing such questions, no less pertinent than difficult, by recalling the distinction implied in the preceding four chapters, involving life, faith, and form. By "life" was meant the concrete reality of the early church as a community of memory and the Spirit; by "faith" was meant the way in which the community explained its reality; and by "form," the outward institutional or organizational structures and procedures the community used to express, conserve, and communicate its life and faith. Now it has been brought out clearly enough, I hope, that these three cannot be separated; we have seen how integral to early Christian life was the primitive faith in Jesus as Lord and Christ; and one has only to recognize that this life was *embodied* in a community to realize that from the beginning some kind of institutional form was involved. Both "life" and "faith" have their more essential and their more formal aspects; and the two are quite inseparable. At the same time, we must recognize that in the beginning unity was more characteristic of life and faith, as spontaneous responses to the event of Christ, than it was of form. This unity of life and faith— which may also be defined as a sharing in a common memory and a common Spirit—may be thought of as implying and promising some kind of common structure; but, as we have seen, this common structure did not emerge in the earliest period. Glimpses or hints of it can be found, and particular features of it are already present; but one must wait till the very end of the second century or the opening years of the third to find it fully and clearly in existence—that is, as fully and clearly in existence as it has ever been. This approximate achievement of institutional unity we were discussing in the closing pages of the preceding chapter.

Now there will be no question about the normative character of early Christian life and faith under their more essential aspect as immediate responses to the event of Christ. There will be no dispute as to the authority of the primitive memory of Jesus and the primitive experience of the Spirit. It is because the New Testament documents embody and express this memory and experience —convey the concrete meaning of the community which constituted the early church—that they *are* the New Testament documents; that is, it was on this account that they were treasured in the church and later canonized. But as regards the more formal and outward aspect of the church's life and faith, what are we to say as to the normativeness of the New Testament period? We have noted in the course of this study not a few common features of order and organization belonging to the New Testament churches, and we have discerned some trends toward a common polity; but, by and large, it must be said that neither the episcopal, the presbyterial, nor yet the congregational structure can be claimed as established in the Apostolic Age. Nor can any formal creedal statement now in use be validated as primitive. If, then, the only historical authority we are to recognize is the authority of the primitive church, we can only say that in the area of polity we lack clear and unmistakable historical authority at every crucial point. The acceptance of the New Testament as our only authority—and as an adequate authority—has the effect of making us, to be sure, inescapably aware of our inward unity, but at the same time it confirms our more outward differences and divisions.

It may be argued that the very fact that the event itself did not produce as an immediate issue a definitive constitution for the church indicates the comparative unimportance of this matter of outward form and also our freedom with respect to it. It is important to acknowledge the truth in this contention. Participation in a common memory, a common Spirit, and a common faith (somewhat as these were defined in the second and third chapters of this book) *does* constitute the essential meaning of the church. The church, however divided outwardly, *does* consist of those who truly share in this community. But we must not fall into the fallacy of thinking of the "more outward" as the *mere* outward—that is, the fallacy of depreciating the significance of the institutional structure of the church. Bishop Newbigin writes:

We can all call to mind movements which have begun as pure upsurges of fresh spiritual vitality, breaking through and revolting against the hardened structure of the older body, and claiming, in the name of the Spirit, liberty from outward forms and institutions. And we have seen how rapidly they develop their own forms, their own structures of thought, of language, and of organization. It would surely be a very unbiblical view of human nature and history to think— as we so often, in our pagan way, do—that this is just an example of the tendency of all things to slide down from a golden age to an age of iron, to identify the spiritual with the disembodied, and to regard visible structure as equivalent to sin. We must rather recognize here a testimony to the fact that Christianity is, in its very heart and essence, not a disembodied spirituality, but life in a visible fellowship, a life which makes such total claim upon us, and so engages our total powers, that nothing less than the closest and most binding association of men with one another can serve its purpose.[4]

If, then, the church is to be united, it must be united in form as well as in Spirit. Visible structure is inevitable in this, as in every human community, and a necessary factor in its cohesiveness. Within limits, to be sure, differences in usage and varieties

[4] Lesslie Newbigin, *The Household of God* (New York: Friendship Press, 1954), pp. 76-77. Used by permission of the publishers.

in organization not only can be tolerated but are to be encouraged. No stiff uniformity is either desirable or, in a living society, conceivable. But there must be a comprehensive and fundamental structure in which all participate. One Spirit implies one body. We must reach some measure of agreement on matters of form as well as of essence if the coming great church is actually to come.

III

But, someone asks, granting that there must be common forms, do we need to rely on the authority of history in developing them? Indeed, you have shown (the questioner continues) that the early church, for all it gives us out of its experience of the event and the Spirit, cannot be depended on as a source of common patterns of order and organization. Almost every contemporary church type can find its warrant in the New Testament—from nonsacramental mysticism to the most realistic sacramentalism, from Pentecostal spiritistic worship to the solemn liturgies, from the most uncompromising independency to the most inflexible hierarchism. It is hopeless, then, to expect agreement on a common structure by returning to the New Testament church. Since this is true, do we not need to get free from the dead hand of the past and deal freshly with the problem of the organization of the coming great church and the ordering of its life, asking what forms will at the present time best express the common life and best serve the common interests?

Here, again, we must acknowledge a certain truth in this contention. The necessary forms of organization and procedure in the united church are not going to be found so long as any large number of us are in the mood to insist that they have been found already—that they are, in fact, strictly identical with the forms now in use in whatever may be our own denomination. The

united church belongs to the future, not to the past; and if anything is clear, it is that the forms of its life have not yet been
finally determined. It would be as certainly false to identify the
coming great church with Roman Catholicism, with Eastern
Orthodoxy, or with Anglicanism as with Lutheranism, Congregationalism, Presbyterianism, Methodism, or any other denominational cult. The united church will be a new creation, and we
should be rash indeed to try artificially to limit the possible
forms it may take.

Still, there are at least two reasons for believing that the forms
of the united church will be, in considerable part, historic forms
—simplified or elaborated or otherwise amended, no doubt, but
still historic forms. One of these reasons lies in the nature of man
as a creature of history. As human beings we belong to our cultural past, and we cannot really and permanently break with it.
No revolution is as radical as it thinks it is, or stays as radical as
it may be at first. The other reason, very closely related, lies in
the nature of the church as being essentially a historical community. The church is not a new thing, or something newly
created whenever the Word is preached and the sacraments administered (though this is true, too, in a sense), but is a great
social body continuously existing through the centuries. I have
used the phrase "new creation" in speaking of the coming great
church; but this phrase in this connection would be quite mis-
leading if it were not understood as referring to the culmination
of a process of creation that began long ago in an event in Palestine and has continued through all the centuries since. The
united church will not be a *new* church; a "new church" could
only be a new denomination. It will be the historic church, puri-
fied, renewed, and fulfilled. The "hand" of the past is not "dead."
If we are held inert and helpless in its grasp, it is because *we* are
dead, not because the past is. The past is a living part of any life

we have. Its hand, far from being dead, beckons us toward any future really possible for us; and we cannot dispense with its guidance. We cannot approach *de novo* the question of structure and form in the united church—whether as regards polity, creed, or liturgy—and expect to reach a common answer. We cannot hope for agreement on this matter as a kind of inevitable expression of the common life, or as a common judgment, freshly arrived at, as to what forms will be most appropriate or practically most useful. The achievement of a united church involves our accepting the authority, in some sense or degree, of historically developed norms of usage and organization.

But these norms the New Testament does not provide. Either, then, we are without historical authority as regards the matters that divide us—and therefore, whether we recognize it or not, without any real hope of overcoming our divisions—or else we cannot limit the locus of this authority to the New Testament period itself. It is my own conviction that we cannot hope for the organic union of Christendom unless the achievements of early Catholicism are taken into account. It may be urged, truly enough, that these achievements do not belong to the *ground* of the church; but they belong to its earliest foundation and therefore to the foundation of any universal visible church actually conceivable within history. We can find the Spirit of the church most authentically in the first century, but no attempt at consolidating the church which skips or bypasses the second century has any chance at success.

If I may quickly cite a quite inadequate but possibly illuminating analogy—such documents as the speeches of Patrick Henry and the Declaration of Independence belong to the "first century" in the history of the American nation and express and convey the spirit of the event in which our country had its birth. But our unity rests just as surely upon the achievements of the several assemblies that finally produced the Constitution in substantially its present form and upon certain early legislative and judicial acts that interpreted and implemented it—all of which belong to what might be called the "second century" of our history. In order to remain united we must return, again and again, to the Revolutionary War period itself, renewing our memory of its events and our participation in its spirit; but we cannot ignore the fact that it was only after the war that what proved to be the abiding institutional forms for the expressing and the implementing of the common life of the emancipated colonies were worked out, and that these forms also have a normative value, a value secondary only to that of the spirit of the original event itself. No one will suspect me of making a comparison, as regards either character or significance, between the beginnings of the nation and the beginnings of the church; and obviously the time spans involved are quite different. But I believe the suggested analogy holds and may help us see that the authority of the ancient church cannot be limited strictly to the New Testament period if the church is ever to be formally united.

IV

Now it is of the greatest importance to recognize that all Christian groups do in fact acknowledge the authority in certain respects of the post-apostolic church. No body of Christians actually "skips or bypasses the second century" and returns directly and freshly to the first. This is true even of those denominations that insist most strenuously upon the New Testament as their only norm. Indeed, it is true in a special sense of them, because the New Testament, which for them carries such exclusive authority, did not exist till the end of the second century and did not take its final form till the end of the fourth. To accept the New Testament means accepting as authoritative not only the several books that compose it but also the acts of the several councils of bishops that determined what the books should be and eventually fixed the limits of the canon. One does not need to acknowledge that the authority of the church councils is of as high an order as the authority of the New Testament books; but the simple fact is that all Christians tacitly accept both. No one proposes that in order to have the true canon we must get back to the canon of the first-century church; we know of course that the first-century church had no canon (that is, of the New Testament). Nor does anyone propose that the question of the contents of the canon should be reopened. As a matter of fact, no one would resist such a suggestion so resolutely as those who insist most strenuously upon the exclusive authority of the primitive church. In other words, the more insistent we are upon the sole normativeness of the New Testament, the more vigorously are we affirming the normativeness of certain decisions of the early Catholic church; and thus we deny our position in seeking to affirm it. The only consistent position is that which recognizes that the New Testament is the creation, not of the first century only, but of the first several centuries of the experience of the church, and that the acceptance of it means the acknowledgment of a broader locus of the authority which ancient Christianity exercises in the church than the primitive community alone comprises.

The commonly accepted creeds of Christendom are also the creation of the post-apostolic church. We have seen that there was from the beginning what can be truly called a common faith, and that this primitive faith (hardly more, or less, than a response to the event) expressed itself in the quasi-creedal assertion that Jesus was Lord and Christ. But so brief and simple a statement was adequate neither for common liturgical confession nor yet for apologetic; and even in the New Testament itself one can see experiments in definition and elaboration.[5] It was not till the middle of the second century, however, that the Old Roman Symbol (the substance of the later Apostles' Creed) emerges as a commonly accepted formulation, and the Nicene Creed was not written till the fourth. Now it cannot be said that all Christian groups acknowledge and use these creeds as formal symbols; but it is an obvious fact that all but a small minority do. It is also true that those who reject them do so because they reject all creeds, not because they have alternative formulations to propose. These creeds represent the church's first achievement of a commonly accepted formulation of its faith and have been in constant use in the worship of the vast majority of Christians for something like sixteen centuries. Even those who do not use the creeds accept, for the most part, their sense (often much more literally than do many who recite them constantly in worship), and thus tacitly acknowledge their authority. But to acknowledge these creeds is to acknowledge the normativeness, in some sense or measure, of the Christianity of the second, third, and fourth centuries. For the definition of the apostles' faith, like the definition of the apostles' writings, was not made by the apostles themselves. The New Testament alone cannot be relied on to justify either. Insofar as we accept the canon (as all of us do) and the ancient creeds (as most of us do), we acknowledge, whether we are aware of doing so or not, the authority of the early Catholic church.

What, then, shall we say of episcopacy? This feature of early Catholic Christianity is also characteristic of much the larger part of Christendom and has been such since the early third century at the latest; for some twelve centuries it was characteristic of all

[5] See O. Cullmann, *Les premières confessions de foi chrétiennes* (Paris: Presses Universitaires de France, 1948), and above, pp. 116-19.

of Christendom. Again, one may ask whether it is really conceivable that there should be a unification of the church which did not involve the universal acceptance of this feature. Certainly it seems most unlikely that the historic episcopate should be given up by those who have it—much more unlikely than that other groups should find it acceptable. Speaking as one born and reared in a denomination where episcopacy in this sense is not known or acknowledged, I must say that when I am thinking seriously and with some attempt at realism, I simply cannot conceive of the union of Christendom except on the ground of a polity which, while not failing to embody the invaluable contributions of groups with a presbyterial or congregational tradition, yet involves the full acceptance of the historic episcopate. I am not speaking of any particular interpretation of its meaning —here great latitude must be permitted—but of the historic episcopate itself. We may agree to disagree with regard to the polity of the church; but if we agree to agree, are we not bound to agree on this historic form? And one may further ask whether we can agree to disagree on so important a matter as the basic organizational structure of the church and have what could, by any stretching of terms, be called an organically united church.

This issue is a thorny one; and it may have been rash for me to raise it, especially so near the end of this book. But having been led to do so by what seems to me to be an inescapable logic, perhaps I shall be pardoned for discussing it somewhat further.

V

At the outset it may be well to recognize as clearly as possible just what the issue is. It is not episcopacy itself. Episcopacy of a very real kind already exists in virtually all our denominations.

The minister of the local church is in many respects a monarchical bishop in the ancient sense. To be sure, he may be chosen or "called" by the congregation, and he may be subject to dismissal by the congregation; but he is not *ordained* by the congregation. His ordination is at the hands of ministers, who in turn were ordained by other ministers. The minister stands in a ministerial succession and is regarded as a minister of the whole church, not of a congregation only or even of a denomination. Moreover, whether we are altogether ready to use the term or not, this succession is thought of as conferring a certain priestly power. Laymen may preach or conduct worship; but in most "churches" only an ordained minister can officiate at the Lord's Supper or unite two persons in holy wedlock. We may think it strange that Ignatius should insist so strongly that there could be no true Eucharist without the bishop (Smyrn. 8) until we remember that there are few modern denominations that do not, at least in practice, take precisely the same position. The crucial issue, then, is not whether we shall have episcopacy simply as such; this we all have, and it is important that we recognize this common possession. The issue is whether we shall accept episcopacy in a special sense: namely, as a distinct order of ministry, superior to the presbyterate and diaconate, and as standing in a particular historic succession. I have said that I see no hope of a united church without the universal acceptance of episcopacy in this historic sense. It seems to me that any objective and realistic appraisal of the actual possibilities must lead to this conclusion. Perhaps it should be added that I am speaking of an acceptance in principle, which may only gradually be implemented, as in the Church of South India, where already ordained ministers of all the constituent bodies have been fully recognized but new ministers are being episcopally ordained. It should also be said (a point to be made again later in this chapter) that this acceptance in principle does not involve commitment in advance to any particular definition of the prerogatives of the bishop or of his administrative functions in the church.

But if so-called Free Churchmen must eventually be willing to accept the historic episcopate, Catholics (if I may use the term to designate those groups which already have it) must be ready to acknowledge the validity and adequacy of their ground for doing so. I do not mean that all conceivable grounds should be thus recognized. I do not see how it would be possible for Catholics to recognize the validity of an acceptance of episcopacy based on merely pragmatic considerations—such as the desire, for example, to increase efficiency in administration or even to promote church union. An acceptance of the historic episcopate based simply on the ground that others have strong convictions as to its indispensability, whereas to us it is a matter of indifference, will not be acceptable to Catholics, and should not be. We shall really accept the historic episcopate only when we accept it with the conviction that there are sound reasons in principle for doing so. As a matter of fact, I do not believe there is any chance of our making even a gesture toward accepting it until we are able to recognize such reasons. When we accept the historic episcopate, as I believe we shall eventually do, it will be because we shall have come to hold a conception of the church and an attitude toward its doctrinal and liturgical tradition which will incline us to accept it. Unless this inner inclination, based in that whole understanding of the church as a visible historical community which we were considering earlier in this chapter,[6] exists, we shall not accept the historic episcopate, no matter how strong the outer, the merely pragmatic, pressures may be. But if it *does* exist, it should be acknowledged as fully validating the acceptance itself.

[6] See pp. 137-39.

This means that the Catholic may need to make some concessions, although I believe he will find that nothing essential in Catholicism needs to be compromised. He must not insist that the only sound reason for accepting episcopacy is the belief that it was the primitive church order or that Jesus or the apostles instituted it. He must not require us to believe that episcopacy constitutes the church (rather than being constituted by it or, at most, with it) —that the essence of the church consists in a priestly hierarchy, above and apart from the community rather than in the community itself, however indispensable a part of it an ordered ministry may be. He must not even demand the belief that episcopacy goes back in uninterrupted succession to the apostles, although it well may. Various particular positions on such issues must, of course, be permitted; but none must be required.

The analogy of canon and creed is instructive here again. All three (that is, canon, creed, and ministry) were regarded by the church of the third century as "apostolic." This means that the early Catholic church, which in reality established these forms (or in whose experience they were first established), thought of itself as doing no more than recognizing what had been established by the apostles themselves. The canon was by definition made up of books written by the apostles; the earliest creed, whether called so at first or not, was the *apostles'* creed; episcopacy was the ministry inaugurated by the apostles and continuing in strict succession from them. But our acceptance of the normative significance of their actions in establishing these forms does not commit us to agreeing with their evaluations of these actions. Our accepting the New Testament canon does not need to mean that we believe all its books were written by apostles; our acceptance of the Apostles' Creed does not need to mean that we think the apostles formulated it, or could have done so; similarly, our acceptance of the historic episcopate in the coming great church must not be made to involve acceptance of either the fact of apostolic succession or of any particular understanding of its meaning. Again, it may be said, one will be free to hold such beliefs, but not to demand them of others.

The Catholic must also be ready to acknowledge the soundness of the historic Protestant emphasis upon a distinction, as regards normative value, between the "first century" and any later century. Something essential is lost if one reduces the authority of the first century to the level of the second, or (what is the same thing) raises the authority of the second to the level of the first. The ultimate norm in Christianity is the event of which the life of the primitive church is the immediate reflection; and the essential being of the church, in the qualitative or concrete sense, as the new community of the Spirit of Christ, was given in that event. But the forms in which the corporate life of this new community would be preserved and expressed in a continuing history were not, in the same complete and definitive way, given in the event, and for the most part had not clearly appeared in the primitive church. It must be recognized, then, that such forms, when they did appear, cannot be thought of as having the same authority as the event and the Spirit. Indeed, it is the event and the Spirit that constantly test and judge them. No later form that was deemed to violate the necessary implications of the event or to be untrue to the essential Spirit of the church could have been tolerated. To be sure, later developments of this kind, in the judgment of great numbers of Christians, did occur; but these never became truly Catholic; indeed, they account for many of the schisms. To attribute authority to any and all forms of faith, worship, and polity adopted by the church or some part of it, without reference to their relation to the event or to the universal Spirit of the church, is to introduce or promote a principle of

146

destruction and of endless division—the one because the other—in the church's life. The Catholic must, in this respect, be "evangelical" in order to be truly Catholic.

Moreover, a way must be found of giving full recognition within the united church to certain values in primitive Christianity which have been preserved and nurtured, perhaps more faithfully and effectively, in denominations of a conciliar or congregational order than in the episcopal bodies. I have in mind here particularly the integrity of the local congregation and its importance as the primary locus of Christian community. No imposed superorganization must be permitted to obscure this importance or to violate this integrity. The historic episcopate is already found in a number of different forms in various communions—Old Catholic, Eastern Orthodox, Roman Catholic, Anglican, Lutheran—involving varying degrees of centralization and power; and new forms can be developed. The Catholic of whatever communion must be willing to dissociate the historic episcopate in the coming great church from his own form or any current form of ecclesiastical polity, or indeed from any form which he, alone or with other Catholics, will be able to devise. Presbyterianism and congregationalism, not to mention other denominational types, will have an indispensable contribution to make to the ultimate form of the church's polity.

The Catholic must also be more eager than he has often been to welcome fresh manifestations of the Spirit, both in preaching and in worship. Although the central place in the corporate life of the coming great church, as was true in the primitive and ancient church, will undoubtedly be held by the sacrament of the Lord's Supper, the great importance of preaching as the inspired proclamation and interpretation of the Word will be fully recognized, and the gift of prophecy will be encouraged and honored. Similarly in worship, while the liturgical treasures of all the great traditions will be laid under tribute and certain liturgical forms will be in universal use, "free" or extempore prayer will also have its place, as it did indeed throughout the early centuries of Christian worship. There is a gift of leadership in prayer as certainly as there is a gift of preaching; and the united church will find ways of utilizing it without detriment either to the order and beauty of common worship or to the sense of its significance as the corporate worship of the universal church. Indeed, such utilization of this gift will have the effect of enhancing the vitality, the beauty, and the meaning of traditional liturgical worship. At the heart of worship is ecstasy; and there are times when no formal prayer can express it. As a matter of fact, our traditional liturgies all contain elements that must originally have had this free, ecstatic character. Who will deny that too rigid liturgical usages, or a too exclusive dependence upon liturgy, have sometimes had the effect of binding or quenching the Spirit?

Nor must the priestly significance of the ministry be so defined as to deny, theoretically or in practice, the freedom of access of the Christian man to the grace of God in Christ. The Catholic is right in saying that there is no access to this grace except through the church; but the church, particularly in this context, must be recognized as being the whole community, not the body of its ministers, which, however indispensable to the form of the church, does not itself constitute the church. The access to God in Christ is available to individuals *within* the church, that is, as members of a living body; not *through* the offices of its ministers in any external or mechanical sense.

But when all these things are said and the precedence of Spirit to form is fully granted, it is still true that, as the one Spirit can express himself fully only in one body, so there can be no united church without certain common forms of polity and worship. And in the absence of established primitive forms, a measure of authority cannot be denied to those later ones which, still early, first achieved universal acceptance in the church, for many centuries enjoyed universal use, and are still characteristic of the larger part of Christendom.

We have seen that this is at least tacitly acknowledged by all of us with respect to canon, and by most of us with respect to creed; and something of the same kind can be said of some of the ancient liturgical usages. We may be less ready to grant that it is true of the historic episcopate also. A part of the reason for this difference will be the mere fact that many of us, familiar with canon and creed, are not used to the episcopal polity and cannot appreciate it from the inside.[7] But there is also a deeper, or at any rate less obvious, ground. While, as we have seen, the canon and the creeds are creations of the church (or creations of God through the church) and, whether we recognize it or not, are accepted by us on the authority of the church, yet both have explicitly to do, not with the church, but with the event. The canon points to the event, comprising by definition those books that were judged to be close to the event, both in time and in meaning; the ancient creeds likewise are concerned with the event, recalling and interpreting it, attempting to formulate the primitive *kerugma* or gospel which proclaimed it. Thus, although the acknowledgment of the authority of the church is *really* implied in our acceptance of the canon and creeds, we may *seem* to be acknowledging only the authority of the event. But as regards the episcopate no such ambiguity is possible. That institution is manifestly concerned, not with the event simply or even primarily, but with the church itself. It is the ancient, and still almost universal, way of saying explicitly what is implied in our acceptance

[7] It should be observed, however, that approximations of the bishop as a diocesan superintendent of churches and even as a "father in God" among the presbyters can be found in many communions even of the congregational type.

of canon and creed: namely, that the Christian church is really one, not only throughout the world but also throughout the centuries; that it derives its character in every place and time not simply from its constituents in that place and time, nor even from the Spirit freshly given, but from the ancient event—and from that event not merely as it is recorded in the New Testament, but as it has been conveyed, for the most part through sacramental and liturgical forms, in the actual life of a continuing historical community; in a word, that historical continuity belongs to the very being of the church.

I would not for a moment suggest that only Christians who belong to episcopally governed churches recognize this fact about the church; such a suggestion would be obviously and utterly untrue. My point is rather that those who recognize this fact about the church most clearly and to whom it is most important will probably not object to the proposal of the historic episcopate for the united church, once that proposal is made in an appropriate form, for the positive reason that they will already have so fully accepted what the historic episcopate properly stands for. The episcopate is the historically developed means and symbol of the unity and continuity of the church. It did in fact arise in response to an effort to affirm this unity and continuity. To argue that this development *had* to take place, whatever the circumstances might have been, because of some inner logic or because in the essential nature of the case the church could not have existed without bishops—as though bishops "carried" the church, rather than the church the bishops—would be, from my point of view, quite false. But it still remains true that, as things actually worked out, the episcopate did become the symbol, because the effective means, of the sacramental unity of the church; and things can never be as though that development had not occurred.

Not infrequently the discussion of this issue turns upon the question whether the historic episcopate belongs to the *esse* or the *bene esse* of the church. I can understand the Catholic's insistence that episcopacy must be recognized as having more than the *bene esse* status. But, on the other hand, there are obvious difficulties in the way of our regarding it as essential. To mention only one: since it cannot be clearly traced to the Apostolic Age and was certainly not generally established then, one cannot say that it belongs to the *esse* of the church without placing in jeopardy the existence of the primitive church itself. Besides, even if the institution of episcopacy could be clearly grounded in the usages of the earliest communities, there would still be the question of whether it was an accidental or an essential feature. If by the *esse* of the church we mean what the church originally was and what it had to be (that is, regardless of the actual historical circumstances in which it arose), then we should have to deny, I think, that episcopacy belongs to the *esse,* any more than do the particular canon we have and the particular creeds we have. All these were gradually developed in response to the actual conditions the church confronted (and these conditions might conceivably have been different). Although all three are in a degree adumbrated in the Apostolic Age (and could not have won later universal acceptance if they had not been), nevertheless none of them, as we have seen, can be thought of as having its origin there. If there is a certain inevitability about these developments, the inevitability exists only in the actual context of history; and if we are trying to define what the church from the very beginning and in the nature of the case *had* to be, we can hardly include episcopacy in our definition. Besides—and most decisively—one may point to the indubitable fact that the reality of the church is actually found, and that manifestly authentic and effective ministries are being actually exercised, in nonepiscopal bodies.

151

But if by the *esse* of the church we mean the *esse* of the coming great church, then the history of the past seventeen or eighteen centuries, and especially of the first two or three of them, becomes an essential element in the definition; and our answer about the status of the historic episcopate may be quite different. Perhaps it is the coming great church which certain Anglican theologians have had in mind when they have spoken of episcopacy as belonging to "the perfection," or, more recently, to "the *plene esse*," of the church.[8] In any case, do we not acknowledge by our use of, and attitude toward, the canon or creed (or both) that not everything which now seems indicated as belonging to the form of the united church had clearly emerged into view by the end of the first century? I for one have no hesitancy in ascribing the same status to episcopacy as to canon and creed, whatever that status should be called. Less than this, I am ready to agree, the Catholic could hardly accept; more than this, I venture to say, he should not ask.

VI

How confidently can we expect the coming great church? How likely is the achievement of the Christian unity we seek? If by "unity" we mean perfect harmony, the complete absence of differences in practice and opinion among Christians, identity of theological emphasis, absolute uniformity in worship, and the like, it is clear that such "unity" not only is impossible but ought not even to be desired—that is, within history. We are not good enough or wise enough to be thus united; it would not do for us to agree perfectly with all others, as it certainly would not do for

---

[8] See the irenic and highly suggestive discussion of this theme in *The Historic Episcopate in the Fullness of the Church,* ed., Kenneth M. Carey (London: The Dacre Press, 1954).

all others to agree perfectly with us. Only in heaven will there be this kind of peace, and only there would it be tolerable. But what shall we say of the possibility of our achieving a more feasible and appropriate kind of unity—a unity allowing for great freedom and many differences, but expressing itself in a single visible body (like the body of a nation) to which all Christians would belong? Even this seems remote; our various divergent traditions are strong and our prejudices even stronger. Some of us find it almost impossible to give others the freedom they must have, and others find it just as hard to acknowledge any curb upon their own freedom; or, to speak more accurately perhaps, both groups prefer the familiar curbs their own denominations impose to the necessarily more generous limits a universal church would prescribe. For actually what often repels us in the idea of the universal church is not the limitations it would place on us but the freedom it would give others—and this is true whether we be Protestant or Catholic. And yet, discouraging as the prospect often seems, who will say that the obstacles to formal unity cannot be overcome? And in a world in which cultural changes are so rapidly occurring, who will want to write off the achievement of a common structure in Christendom as being, even humanly speaking, an impossibility?

But this achievement when it comes will not be a human achievement. "Unless the Lord builds the house, those who build it labor in vain." (Ps. 127:1.) Although we shall be used in the construction of this "holy temple in the Lord," this "dwelling place of God in the Spirit" (Eph. 2:21-22), it will not be the consequence of our shrewd planning, of our cautious concessions and careful compromises. It will be God's building—both the plan and the execution will be his—and we shall be not so much builders of it as "built into it," as the writer to the Ephesians says (2:22). Our part in the building will be allowing ourselves to be "built in," yielding ourselves without reservation—without care for a single vested interest, without self-righteous fidelity to a single ancient prejudice—to the mighty working of the Spirit, who alone can break down all dividing walls of hostility and can reconcile us all to God in one body.

But although this consummation will represent a new work of the Spirit—the work of the Spirit is always new—it will involve a return to the past. The Spirit, however new his work, is not a new Spirit. He is the Spirit of an ancient event and of a historical community. The same writer who reminds us so impressively that the united church will be a living thing which only God can make can also speak of it as "built upon the foundation of the apostles and prophets" (Eph. 2:20). The coming great church will not be a novel thing created by our enthusiasm any more than it will be the same old thing patched up by our industry and ingenuity. It will be a fresh work of the same Spirit who has been working hitherto; and the new church will be the old fulfilled.

The return to the past will not be simply a return to the primitive church. What we seek is the fulfillment of a historical process, not the restoration of a particular historical situation. No particular historical situation, as a matter of fact, is worthy of being restored, not even the situation of the early church, which partakes of the same limited and faulty character as does the church in every subsequent period. But apart from this bearing of the general truth, it must be recognized that the very features of primitive Christianity that make it an indispensable resource keep it from being an adequate norm. Primitive Christianity represents an immediate response to the event of Christ, and only within its life can the event be found in its pristine power. But this response could be as complete as it was and the meaning of the event could be so powerfully felt and communicated partly because the early church conceived of itself as standing at the very end of history.

It could be so completely preoccupied with the event partly because that event was, quite literally, the final event. The most primitive Christianity had no thought of surviving within history and no interest in developing forms of survival. It was like a nation suddenly brought into being by some great crisis and knowing the concrete meaning of that crisis as no later generation will know it, but thus far without constitution or government, without a flag or a song.

There must be a return to what is essential in the life of the primitive church—to the event in which it was born and the Spirit which made it a distinctive living community. But there must also be a return to what is essential in the Catholicism which, adumbrated in the first century, clearly emerged only later. To discern what is "essential" in both primitive and Catholic Christianity will require of both Catholic and Protestant a degree of critical intelligence and spiritual sensitivity, of willingness to listen to others in humility and love, of devotion to the truth and to Christ, which goes beyond anything either has thus far attained. But the discernment of both "essentials" is itself essential if the church is ever to be united. The coming great church will be apostolic as well as Catholic, and Catholic as well as apostolic. Only by seeking to be both can the church learn the true meaning of being either, and thus become what it truly is, holy and one.

INDEX